maps

on the road with fodor's

A TRIP TAKES YOU OUT OF YOURSELF. Concerns of life at home completely disappear, driven away by more immediate thoughts—about, say, what marvels will beguile the next day, or where you'll have dinner. That's where Fodor's comes in. We make sure that you know all your options, so that you don't miss something that's around the next bend just because you didn't know it was there. Mindful that the best memories of your trip might have nothing to do with what you came to Aruba to see, we guide you to sights large and small all over the island. You might set out to relax in the sun on Eagle Beach, but back at home you find yourself unable to forget the breathtaking rock formation at Natural Bridge or the caves once inhabited by ancient peoples in Arikok National Park. With Fodor's at your side, serendipitous discoveries are never far away.

About Our Writers

Our success in showing you every corner of Aruba is a credit to our extraordinary writers. Although there's no substitute for travel advice from a good friend who knows your style, our contributors are the next best thing—the kind of people you would poll for travel advice if you knew them.

New York–based **Karen W. Bressler** escaped the northeastern winter to interview local celebrities in Aruba and tour their beautiful island. After clubbing at E Zone and dipping her toes in

Fodor's POCKET

aruba

second edition

fodor's travel publications
new york • toronto • london • sydney • auckland
www.fodors.com

contents

the calm waters of Baby Beach, she set about compiling this exciting guidebook—and updating it for us this year—which she hopes will convey Aruba as "one happy island." On her most recent visit, she was interviewed on Aruban television about her island experiences. Karen has written for *Condé Nast Traveler*, *Bride's*, *Bridal Guide*, *Elegant Bride*, and *Honeymoon* magazines and writes regularly for *Elite Traveler* and *Ocean Drive*. She has also contributed to *Fodor's Brazil*, *Fodor's Caribbean*, and *Fodor's Israel*, and has published several books including *Workout on the Go*, *A Century of Lingerie*, *Yoga Baby*, *D.I.Y. Beauty*, and *The Hair Bible*.

Elise Rosen—who worked side by side with Karen Bressler— has been a reporter for the Associated Press in New York and Los Angeles and a producer for Time Warner's cable station, NY1 News. She is currently a financial editor in New York. Her articles have appeared in publications throughout the United States and as far away as Saudi Arabia. Elise also has been an editorial contributor to several books, including *Fodor's Caribbean*, *Fodor's Israel*, *Career Opportunities in Art*, and *America's Elite 1000*.

None of the elected officials **Suzanne Bressler** met during her years working at New York's City Hall were quite as "happy" as Aruba's minister of economic affairs and tourism. Is it any wonder? One day of island life put that burning question to rest. Suzanne has also reported on banking legislation from Capitol Hill and has written on behalf of *Worldbusiness* magazine. She is

Your Checklist for a Perfect Journey

WAY AHEAD

- Devise a trip budget.
- Write down the five things you want most from this trip. Keep this list handy before and during your trip.
- Make plane or train reservations. Book lodging and rental cars.
- Arrange for pet care.
- Check your passport. Apply for a new one if necessary.
- Photocopy important documents and store in a safe place.

A MONTH BEFORE

- Make restaurant reservations and buy theater and concert tickets. Visit fodors.com for links to local events.
- Familiarize yourself with the local language or lingo.

TWO WEEKS BEFORE

- Replenish your supply of medications.
- Create your itinerary.
- Enjoy a book or movie set in your destination to get you in the mood.

- Develop a packing list. Shop for missing essentials. Repair and launder or dry-clean your clothes.

A WEEK BEFORE

- Stop newspaper deliveries. Pay bills.
- Acquire traveler's checks.
- Stock up on film.
- Label your luggage.
- Finalize your packing list— take less than you think you need.
- Create a toiletries kit filled with travel-size essentials.
- Get lots of sleep. Don't get sick before your trip.

A DAY BEFORE

- Drink plenty of water.
- Check your travel documents.
- Get packing!

DURING YOUR TRIP

- Keep a journal/scrapbook.
- Spend time with locals.
- Take time to explore. Don't plan too much.

currently editing the StartFresh.com kosher diet Web site, which allows her to savor things as sweet as her memories of Aruba.

You can rest assured that you're in good hands—and that no property mentioned in the book has paid to be included. Each has been selected strictly on its merits, as the best of its type in its price range.

We'd like to thank everyone at the Aruba Hotel and Tourism Authority; Antonio Leo and the Aruba Tourism Authority; and friendly Aruban, Ito Tromp. Thanks also go to Barry and Sheila Weintrob, whose Goodwill Ambassadorships (given to visitors of 20 consecutive years) are just around the corner.

Don't Forget to Write

Your experiences—positive and negative—matter to us. If we have missed or misstated something, we want to hear about it. We follow up on all suggestions. Contact the Aruba editor at editors@fodors.com or c/o Fodor's at 1745 Broadway, New York, New York 10019. And have a fabulous trip!

Karen Cure

Karen Cure
Editorial Director

THE BAHAMAS

Turks and Caicos Islands

Cuba

Haiti

Dominican Republic

Hispaniola

Port-au-Prince

Santo Domingo

Jamaica

GREATER

ANTI

N

Caribbean

0		200 miles
0		300 km

Aruba

Willemstad

Curaçao

Bon

VENEZUELA

COLOMBIA

Maracaibo

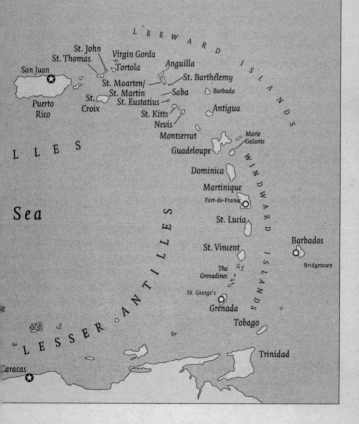

ATLANTIC OCEAN

LEEWARD ISLANDS

St. John
St. Thomas
Virgin Gorda
Tortola
Anguilla
San Juan
St. Barthélemy
St. Maarten/
St. Martin
Saba
Barbuda
Puerto
Rico
St. Eustatius
St. Croix
St. Kitts
Antigua
Nevis
Montserrat
Marie Galante
Guadeloupe
WINDWARD ISLANDS
Dominica
Martinique
Fort-de-France
L L E S
St. Lucia
Barbados
Sea
St. Vincent
Bridgetown
A N T I L L E S
The Grenadines
St. George's
L E S S E R
Grenada
Tobago
Caracas
Trinidad

aruba

The small crowd inside the main lounge of the cruise ship, which has just docked this morning, includes government officials and the press. They listen as the minister of tourism warmly greets the crew. Flashbulbs reflect off newly shined mirrors and bottles of champagne as the captain takes center stage. "I sailed to Aruba every week for almost 25 years, but that was a long time ago. I can't tell you how good it is to be back; now I know I'm home again."

In This Chapter

introducing aruba

FLAIR IS AN ARUBAN HALLMARK—flair for language, music, food, hospitality, storytelling, and, above all, for life. You'll notice this joie de vivre as you meander through the streets or mingle with locals in a bar. Perhaps you'll revel in it as you paint the town red, dine at a fine restaurant, kick back at your hotel, or soak up the sun on a beach. Aruba's slogan sums it up best; this is, indeed, "One Happy Island."

The "A" in the ABC Islands (the other two being Bonaire and Curaçao), tiny Aruba got its name from the Arawak word *oruba* (well placed), as it was convenient to South America. The conquistadors also found it a good jumping-off point for the Spanish Main, which held the promise of gold. They called the island *oro hubo*. There was gold, although it wasn't found until many years after the conquistadors first arrived. Today both meanings hold true—Aruba is both a place of golden sunny days and a convenient vacation destination where golden memories are made.

Once a member of the Netherlands Antilles, the island became an independent entity within the Netherlands in 1986. Throughout its history Aruba's economy has relied on horse trading, gold (discovered here in 1824) mining, aloe vera cultivating, and refining Venezuelan oil. These days, however, tourism is the primary industry, and the island's population of 95,000 treats visitors as valued guests. The national anthem proclaims, "The greatness of our people is their great cordiality," and this is no exaggeration. Waiters serve you with smiles, English is spoken everywhere, and hotel hospitality directors appear delighted to fulfill your needs.

With its low humidity, average temperature of 28°C (82°F), modest rainfall, and location below the hurricane belt, Aruba seems like paradise. Silky sands and cooling trade winds have made the calm southwest coast a tourist mecca. Most of the island's 28 major hotels—with on-site restaurants, boutiques, and casinos—sit side by side down a single strip of shore. Every night sees theme parties, treasure hunts, beachside barbecues, and fish fries with steel bands or dancers. Surround all this with warm blue-green waters and you've got the perfect destination for anyone who wants sun salted with lots of activities. Courteous service, efficient amenities, modern casinos, glorious beaches, duty-free shopping, and remarkably varied cuisine help fill Aruba's more than 7,500 hotel rooms.

THE MAKING OF ARUBA

THE PEOPLE

Aruba's first inhabitants were the Caiquetio people of the Arawak tribe (the earliest relics of their existence date from 2500 BC), who migrated from South America to avoid clashes with the more aggressive Caribs. The Arawaks formed a peaceful tribal society, living in small family groups subsisting on fish and making rudimentary tools from shells and stones. As their civilization developed, they turned to farming. Recent excavations in the Santa Cruz area have unearthed remnants of vessel pottery— cooking pots, baking griddles, burial urns, and other finely polished and painted pieces—and fragments of wooden house posts that indicate sophisticated design and manufacturing techniques. Inscriptions from about AD 1000 are still visible in Aruba's limestone caves.

In about 1499 Spanish explorer Alonso de Ojeda (a lieutenant of Christopher Columbus) was the first European to land on the

Islandscapes

Aruba's topography is unusual for a Caribbean island. The southern and western coasts consist of miles of palm-lined, white-sand beaches. The calm, blue-green waters are so clear that in some areas visibility extends to a depth of 30 m (100 ft). The northeast coast is wild and rugged; here the waves pound against the coral cliffs, creating remarkable rock formations. The desert-like interior is home to various types of cacti and still more extraordinary rock formations. And everywhere, divi-divi trees flourish.

Set in the Caribbean Sea, Aruba is at latitude 12°30′ north and longitude 70° west and lies about 32 km (20 mi) from Venezuela's northern coast, near the Península Paraguaná. It's a small island, only 32 km (20 mi) long and 10 km (6 mi) across at its widest point, with a total area of 180 square km (70 square mi).

In the east, Arikok National Park makes up 18% of the island's total area. In the park is the 188-m (617-ft) Mt. Yamanota, Aruba's highest peak. The capital, Oranjestad, is on the southwest coast. Here Dutch and Spanish influences are evident in the colorful houses along Wilhelminastraat. Two main thoroughfares—J. E. Irausquin and L. G. Smith boulevards—link the capital to the hotels along Eagle and Palm beaches.

To the southeast lies San Nicolas, the island's second largest metropolis and the site of an oil refinery. At Aruba's northwestern tip are large rolling sand dunes as well as the island's newest golf course. Nestled at the island's heart, Santa Cruz is the cradle of religious culture, symbolized by a large cross marking the spot where Spanish missionaries introduced Christianity.

island. According to oral history, an Arawak chieftain guided the first Spanish arrivals inland, where they erected a cross to mark the occasion. (In 1968 this event was commemorated by the placement of a large wooden cross atop a rocky hill in Santa Cruz.) Believing there were no precious metals—alluvial gold wasn't found until 1824—the conquerors exported the entire Arawak population in 1515 to Hispaniola (today's Dominican Republic and Haiti) to work in the copper mines. Though some were allowed to return after 1527, when Spain began actively to colonize Aruba, Bonaire, and Curaçao, the mass abduction ended much of the Arawak culture on the island.

In 1636, during the Eighty Years' War between Holland and Spain, the Dutch took control of Aruba, Bonaire, and Curaçao, ruling them under the charter of the Dutch West India Company. Over the next 100 years, commerce grew on the island, which served as a satellite to the administrative center on larger Curaçao.

Owing to the arid climate and poor soil, Aruba was spared from plantation economics and the slave trade; instead, the Dutch used the remaining Arawaks to herd cattle. The Dutch held power until 1805, when the English laid claim to Aruba briefly during the Napoleonic Wars. The Dutch Republic on the European continent had fallen to the French in 1795, and France annexed the Netherlands in 1810. But after Napoléon's defeat in 1815, political lines throughout Europe were redrawn. The Kingdom of the Netherlands was born, and in 1816 possession of Aruba was returned permanently to the Dutch.

In 1750, Domingo Antonio Silvestre—who had been converted to Catholicism by Spanish missionaries—built a small chapel at Alto Vista on the island's north shore to accommodate the Catholic community, which until this time had had no formal place of worship. The winding approach road is lined with 12 white crosses indicating the stations of the cross, which pilgrims can follow to the tranquil chapel. The church of Santa Ana, built in the district of Noord in 1776, is renowned for its handsomely carved oak altar, which was awarded a prize for neo-Gothic design at the Rome exhibition of 1870.

The first Protestant church was built in 1848 in the center of Oranjestad. The original building houses a Bible museum and is maintained by the congregation; an adjoining larger church is used for weekly services. Another landmark house of worship, the Inmaculada Concepción church in Santa Cruz, is noted for the colorful biblical mural decorating its nave. The Beth Israel synagogue was built in 1962 to meet the needs of the growing Jewish community. (Its members originally arrived in the 1920s, when an international workforce was drawn to Aruba to staff the oil refinery.)

With a history full of cultures clashing and melding, it's no surprise that most islanders are fluent in several languages. School lessons are taught in Dutch, the official language. Arubans begin studying English, recognized as the international tongue, beginning in the fourth grade. Spanish, essential due to Aruba's proximity to South America, is taught in school as early as fifth grade, and French is offered as an option in high school. In normal conversation, however, the locals speak Papiamento—a mix of Spanish, Dutch, Portuguese, English, and French, as well as Indian and African languages. Since 1998, Papiamento has also been taught in grade school.

THE ECONOMY

Early on, Aruba's main source of income was drawn from exporting horses—brought in by the Spanish and bred on the island—to Jamaica and Cuba. In the 16th century, Aruba was a free-roaming horse ranch. There were no European settlements other than garrisons until the 19th century. Later, the island's Arawak population herded cattle that were traded or sold to Curaçao and made glass objects to sell. The first white colonists arrived from Curaçao in 1754, and several merchant families followed. Many who settled here in the 18th century worked in

Venezuela as seasonal laborers on coffee and cocoa plantations; others headed for Jamaica and Cuba. Then in 1824 the discovery of gold on the island's northern slopes at Rooi Fluit boosted the economy. Intermittent reports of gold finds led several exploration companies to set up shop, until the gold was exhausted and the related businesses ceased operations in 1916.

Another major revenue source was the cultivation of aloe (raw sap from the plant was used as a laxative). By the 1920s Aruba was responsible for 70% of the world's aloe supply, with England accounting for most of the intake. The crop brought in about $1 million per year. Calcium phosphate was also a source of income; it was mined in Aruba from 1879 to 1914 and exported to Europe and the United States.

But it was oil that ultimately fueled Aruba's economic boom. In 1924, the Lago refinery was built in San Nicolas. Searching for a hospitable seaport and a stable political climate in which to process the oil from Venezuela's Lake Maracaibo fields, the Standard Oil Company of New Jersey (later Exxon) took over the refinery in 1932. It was soon producing 440,000 barrels of refined oil a day. The company hired thousands of North Americans, Arubans, and other Caribbean islanders, and San Nicolas thrived as residential and commercial areas sprang up to accommodate the workforce.

The refinery played an integral role in World War II, producing one in every 16 gallons of motor fuel used by the Allies. A German submarine had orders to destroy the refinery in 1942 but was unable to fire its cannons. Historians theorize that this failure was one of the events that tipped the hand of victory toward the Allies. By 1949 the refinery employed 8,300 people—roughly 16% of the populace. Indeed, Aruba's population grew sixfold in the three decades after the refinery was built, surging from 9,000 in 1924 to 54,000 in 1954.

Due to an unstable oil market, however, the refinery was closed in 1985. Although the Coastal Corporation of Texas reopened it in 1991 (and it now produces 150,000 barrels a day), the tourist trade has replaced oil as Aruba's primary source of income. Education, health care, and other public services are financed by tourism, which has also helped to keep the unemployment rate at less than 1%. Because of this, it's no surprise that guests are warmly received. This warmth has, in turn, contributed to an increase in visitors—from 206,750 in 1985 to 721,224 in 2000.

THE GOVERNMENT

Until late 1985 Aruba was a member of the Netherlands Antilles, along with Bonaire, Curaçao, St. Maarten, St. Eustatius, and Saba. On January 1, 1986, Aruba was granted a new status as an independent entity within the Kingdom of the Netherlands, which now consists of the Netherlands, the Netherlands Antilles, and Aruba.

The island has a royally appointed governor, who acts as the Dutch sovereign's representative for a six-year term. Executive power is held by the seven-member council of ministers, appointed by the legislative council for four-year terms and presided over by the prime minister, who is elected every four years. The legislature consists of a parliament whose 21 members are elected by popular vote to serve a four-year term. Legal jurisdiction lies with the Common Court of Justice of Aruba and the Netherlands Antilles as well as the Supreme Court of Justice at the Hague in the Netherlands. Defense and foreign affairs still fall under the realm of the kingdom, while internal matters involving such things as customs, immigration, aviation, and communications are handled autonomously.

THE LANGUAGE

Papiamento is a unique Creole language—a mellifluous blend of African, European, and Arawak tongues—that's widely spoken on Aruba, Bonaire, and Curaçao. One theory holds that Papiamento originated on Curaçao in the 17th century to afford a means of communication between African slaves and their Dutch owners.

"Go on with the Struggle"

Arubans are proud of their autonomous standing within the Kingdom of the Netherlands, and it's Gilberto François "Betico" Croes who is heralded as the hero behind the island's status aparte (separate status). His birthday, January 25, is an official Aruban holiday.

During the Dutch colonial expansion of the 17th century, Aruba and five other islands—Bonaire, Curaçao, St. Maarten, St. Eustatius, and Saba— became territories known as the Netherlands Antilles. After World War II, these islands began to pressure Holland for autonomy, and in 1954 they became a collective self-governing entity under the umbrella of the Kingdom of the Netherlands.

At this time, there were several political parties in power on the island. Soon, however, Juancho Irausquin (who has a major thoroughfare named in his honor) formed a new party that maintained control for nearly two decades. Irausquin was considered the founder of Aruba's new economic order and the forebear of modern Aruban politics. After his death, his party's power diminished.

In 1971 Croes, then a young, ambitious school administrator, became the leader of another political party. Bolstered by a thriving economy generated by Aruba's oil refinery, Croes spearheaded the island's cause to secede from the Netherlands Antilles and to gain status as an equal partner within the Dutch kingdom. Sadly, he didn't live to celebrate the realization of his dream. On December 31, 1985, the day before Aruba's new status became official, Croes was in a car accident that put him in a coma for 11 months. He died on November 26, 1986. Etched in the minds of Arubans are his prophetic words: "Si mi cai na cominda, gara e bandera y sigui cu e lucha" ("If I die along the way, seize the flag and go on with the struggle").

Another holds that the language developed somewhat earlier, blending the tongues of the Spanish settlers and the indigenous population. In either case, words and phrases were soon borrowed from still other peoples, including Portuguese and Spanish missionaries and South American traders. Still later, it was peppered with some English and French elements.

Linguists believe the name Papiamento (a variation of Papiamentu) probably derives from the Portuguese verb *papiar*, meaning "to chatter." In Papiamento, as in some other Creole languages, the verb *papia* means "to speak." Add the suffix *mentu*, which means "the way of doing something" and you form a noun. Thus, Papiamento is roughly translated as "the way of speaking." (Sometimes the suffix -*mentu* is spelled in the Spanish and Portuguese way [-*mento*], creating the variant spelling.)

Papiamento began as an oral tradition, handed down through the generations and spoken by all social classes. On Aruba, you'll hear a lilting tone to the language, while on Curaçao, the delivery is more rapid-fire. In Bonaire, the sound is somewhere in between. There's no uniform spelling or grammar from island to island or even from one neighborhood to another.

In 1995 Aruba's citizens began a grassroots effort to raise awareness of Papiamento and to have it taught in the schools. It was made part of the curriculum in 1998; that year was also declared the Year of Papiamento on Aruba. With its official recognition, Papiamento continues to be refined and standardized.

PORTRAITS

TOURISM MINISTER FACES NEW CHALLENGES

Edison "Eddy" Briesen has returned as Aruba's minister of economic affairs and tourism after residents flirted briefly with another party's rule. They essentially asked him back. As

Papiamento Primer

Arubans enjoy it when visitors use their language, so don't be shy. You can buy a Papiamento dictionary to build your vocabulary, but here are a few pleasantries—including some terms of friendship and love—to get you started:

BON DIA.	Good morning.
BON TARDI.	Good afternoon.
BON NOCHI.	Good evening/night.
BON BINI.	Welcome.
AJO.	Bye.
TE AWORO.	See you later.
PASA UN BON DIA.	Have a good day.
DANKI.	Thank you.
NA BO ORDO.	You're welcome.
CON TA BAI?	How are you?
MI TA BON.	I am fine.
BAN GOZA!	Let's enjoy!
PABIEN!	Congratulations!
QUANTO COSTA ESAKI?	How much is this?
HOPI BON	Very good
AMI	Me
ABO	You
NOS DOS	The two of us
MI DUSHI	My sweetheart
KU TUR MI AMOR	With all my love
UN SUNCHI	A kiss
UN BRAZA	A hug
RANKA LENGA	To French kiss
MI STIMA ARUBA.	I love Aruba.

minister of economic affairs, he's responsible for the country's economic, social, and cultural well-being. As minister of tourism, he's responsible for the growth of the industry. Under his initial leadership, between 1989 and 1994, the number of arrivals increased substantially. He has a half decade of experience directing Aruba's public transportation company, Arubus, and has also served as a member of Parliament. Also a very active chair of the Caribbean Tourism Organization, his combined political and management background and hands-on experience make him perhaps the best equipped to face the island's new challenges. We caught up with him soon after he finished moving his files back into the office, and here's what he had to tell us.

FODOR'S: How has your job changed since you were last in office?

BRIESEN: First of all, the minister of economic affairs is now also the minister of tourism, which means that the two areas will now receive the cross-referencing of initiatives that makes sense, since both areas are inherently interwoven. Second, we find ourselves in a bit of a different tourism environment in the world right now, particularly after the events of September 11, 2001. When the United States economy starts to slide, the Aruban tourism industry shifts downward, too. We will need to invest more in our public relations efforts to remind potential visitors that we are not far from home and that we are quite secure.

FODOR'S: What makes Aruba a safe place to vacation?

BRIESEN: We have an overall sense of peace and security, especially due to the U.S. Air Force presence nearby on Curaçao. And specifically, our crime rate is down, and Arubans are tourist-friendly, which means they work hard to ensure that visitors have what they need and are safe wherever they are. The fact that Aruba is more like a domestic flight from the United States than other destinations abroad may also make a visit here less troubling in terms of air travel.

FODOR'S: What makes you most proud of your island?

BRIESEN: The people of Aruba are what make me the most proud of our island. The friendliness is outstanding. Aruba lives with its doors open. There are no appointments necessary. There's a saying about how before your guests can even honk their horns to let you know they are pulling up to your home, they are already in your living room. That describes the prevailing attitude on Aruba. Also, our children learn up to five different languages in school and at home, so we are able to converse and interact with so many, whether they speak French, English, Spanish, German, Dutch, or even Papiamento. That makes us a very versatile host for tourists and an effective member of international conversations when we interface with other tourist nations and prevailing economic powers.

FODOR'S: Do you have a story of a special encounter with a tourist or of a tourist who has touched your life?

BRIESEN: Once on a day off, a friend and I came across some tourists stranded on the side of the road, so we stopped to help them. Their car was a rental, so while waiting for the rental company to come to their aid we managed to get the car to my friend's house to keep it off the road and out of the way. The driver offered me a tip, which of course, I refused. Instead, he gave me his business card and said if there was ever a way he could help me, I should let him know. In return, I gave him my business card, too. He was pretty surprised when he saw what I did for a living, and the moment instantly became memorable!

FODOR'S: What are your own favorite places to visit on Aruba?

BRIESEN: I particularly like the Natural Bridge, and smaller beaches that are not as crowded as some others. We have some beautiful, quiet beaches with long stretches of white sand.

FODOR'S: What's your favorite local hangout? Where do you go on your day off?

BRIESEN: I spend a lot of time going to events, so on my day off, as most Arubans do, I spend time with my family. Arubans stick to family on Sundays. Family ties are very important and time spent with family has diminished over the last few years, as more young Arubans go to study abroad and become independent at an early age. So we make the most of family time while we can.

FODOR'S: What are some recent changes that will make your job easier this time around?

BRIESEN: There are a lot more new facilities now than there were six or seven years ago. There's a new air and water plant, which is great for both the environment and tourism, and there is a higher level of cleanliness and service. Some facilities, like golf course facilities, have expanded. We want to continue expanding our facilities, and then later, we can look at expanding our hotels. First we want to ensure that our occupancy rates are at 75% and higher, and find ways to attract more tourists so that the economy will follow. With these advances we can then invest more money in economic development around the island.

FODOR'S: What are some of the newer challenges you will face?

BRIESEN: One of the larger challenges we will face is making sure people are comfortable, and that they feel how safe it is to travel and stay here. We will have to work to turn around the negative aspects of what has happened on the global terrorism front. Another is not to lose our Aruban identity and our inherent attitude toward tourism as we draw labor from abroad. It is important to promote the awareness of our tourism industry in education, by including it in our school curriculum to show kids its importance as the driving force of our economy.

FODOR'S: What changes do you hope to see in Aruba in the next 10 years?

BRIESEN: We aim to improve the telecommunications system for our tourists. We also plan to expand facilities to provide more

Distance Conversion Chart

KILOMETERS/MILES

To change kilometers (km) to miles (mi), multiply km by .621.

To change mi to km, multiply mi by 1.61.

KM TO MI	MI TO KM
1=.62	1=1.6
2=1.2	2=3.2
3=1.9	3=4.8
4=2.5	4=6.4
5=3.1	5=8.1
6=3.7	6=9.7
7=4.3	7=11.3
8=5.0	8=12.9

METERS/FEET

To change meters (m) to feet (ft), multiply m by 3.28.

To change ft to m, multiply ft by .305.

M TO FT	FT TO M
1=3.3	1=.30
2=6.6	2=.61
3=9.8	3=.92
4=13.1	4=1.2
5=16.4	5=1.5
6=19.7	6=1.8
7=23.0	7=2.1
8=26.2	8=2.4

extensive options for activities and entertainment. We will continue, hopefully, to serve our visitors with the friendliness, warmth, and level of sincerity that has become our trademark as an island and as a competitive vacation destination. So we won't be making any changes that take away from our ability to be involved with our visitors. For example, I recently discussed a suggested need to improve our street and road signs around the island. The development professional with whom I was speaking disagreed with the suggestion, stating that tourists should always feel they can stop local people and ask questions. Talk to an Aruban and he will point you in the right direction.

A CABBIE'S ROAD TO FRIENDSHIP

Janchi Hart, a local taxi driver, was once approached by an American cruise-ship passenger who needed a ride to the hospital to visit her husband, who had broken his ankle. As a result of Hart's friendly, accommodating manner, the visitor hired him to take her around the island throughout her stay. After she and her husband returned home, Hart called the couple to see how they had managed in their travels. They were so touched by this gesture that they began a correspondence and have since visited him and his family in Aruba.

As a result of his extra efforts, Hart won an award from the Aruba Quality Foundation and was asked to represent the island at a dinner celebrating friendship in Chicago on New Year's Eve, 1999. He and his wife joined tourism representatives from all over the world in festivities complete with fireworks and a city tour.

Hart continues to drive his taxi and remains unfazed by such typical tourist questions as "How's the weather?" and "How many miles is it to the hotel?" He says he likes his job because he meets different kinds of people every day, but he could do without the traffic caused by the island's 400 cabs. Still, with so many taxis, it's no wonder that Hart and his compatriots are always at your service.

A yellow-bellied barika geel lands on the table and glares enviously at the buffet breakfast of muffins, mangoes, and berries. The waves glisten in the background and the sun lights up his colorful feathers as he flutters impatiently and staggers around, trying to plan his next move. Even the seagulls gliding overhead can't divert the little guy's attention. Someone puts a morsel of food in front of him; he eagerly grabs it before flying off into the warm air of another perfect Aruban day.

In This Chapter

perfect days and nights

ARE YOU PERPLEXED ABOUT WHICH OF ARUBA'S MANY BEACHES is best or about how to spend your time during one of the island's rare rainy days? Below are some suggestions to guide you. There are also a few ideas on how to spend a night (or two) celebrating all the perfect days you've been having.

A PERFECT DAY AT THE BEACH

Aruba's white sands and turquoise waters are legendary, but for perfection, head to the island's southernmost tip, where the beaches are the most secluded. Just make sure you wear plenty of sunscreen; the cooling trade winds can be deceiving.

Before setting out, rent snorkel gear at your hotel so that you can fully appreciate the calm water and all its inhabitants. And why not pack a picnic? Many hotels will prepare one at your request, or you can stop by a supermarket (there are several on L. G. Smith Boulevard) to pick up provisions for the day.

The Kadushi Juice Bar at the foot of the beachfront pool area at the Hyatt Regency Aruba is a great place to start your day. Slowly sip a fruit or veggie smoothie as you relax on a lounge chair overlooking the waves. From here, make the 27-km (17-mi) trip by rental car southeast to Baby Beach, which is as placid as a wading pool and just about as shallow (only 4–5 ft deep). The shady, thatched areas that dot its powdery sands are ideal for cooling off.

Splash about in the water and do a little snorkeling. Try your hand at a game of paddleball or Frisbee (buy or rent equipment before setting out). In the afternoon, sack out on the sand and get some well-deserved rest. After all, you're on vacation. Be sure to wake up in time for happy hour (it starts at 5 PM) at Coco Restaurant, an eight-minute walk northwest of Baby Beach. There's often live entertainment here; regardless, it's a great place to grab a rum punch and chill.

A PERFECT RAINY DAY

Aruba has a reputation for guaranteed sunshine because of its location outside the hurricane belt. But weather patterns can be unpredictable. Here's what to do if you get caught in a storm.

Have breakfast at DeliFrance in the Certified Mega Mall on L. G. Smith Boulevard. The freshly baked bagels and the hot Dutch pancakes covered in powdered sugar will surely warm you up. By 10 or so, head to downtown Oranjestad's Archaeological Museum, where you'll find a vast collection of Arawak artifacts, farm and domestic utensils, and skeletons. Spend an hour walking around, and you'll get a taste of Aruban history. Another option is the Eagle Bowling Palace, which has 16 lanes, a cocktail lounge, and a snack bar. You'll never know how frightful the weather is outside.

For lunch, head to the pool bar at the Divi Aruba Beach Resort, where the brick oven cooks up the island's tastiest pizzas. Make-your-own-daiquiri machines wait for you to fulfill your bartending fantasies. The canopy over the bar will shield you from the rain, and the people on the bar stools beside you will no doubt swap stories with you (and maybe even drinks) or start singing songs.

After lunch, treat yourself to a massage. Try the Mandara Spa at the Marriott Aruba Ocean Club, which offers Swedish, sports-reflexology, and aromatherapy massages (50 minutes, $85–$100; share with another for $155–$180). Your body will thank you. Your soul will, too. Stick around to luxuriate in the spa's mint-oil scented steam room and pick up a pot of bio-active foot balm to carry the experience into your post-vacation days. You might also want to hop in a cab and head for the airport to extend your airline ticket (in hopes of a few more sunny days). Wrap up your rainy day with an early evening movie at the Seaport Cinema in the Seaport Village Market Place. Its six theaters show the latest from Hollywood.

A PERFECT NIGHT OF ROMANCE

When the sun goes down, Aruba becomes one of the most romantic settings on earth. Here's how to share it with that special someone.

Make reservations at Brisas Del Mar, which is always packed at sunset. Ask for a table on the terrace, where the breeze is inviting and the ocean view is mesmerizing. If you're lucky, the long-time owner will join you for a bit and tell wonderful stories of past guests. Be careful what you say—you may end up in one of these tales.

Have dinner at Le Dôme, another place where reservations are required. Service doesn't get any better than this; neither does food. Share a delectable French dish, dive into a dessert for two, order some coffee, and cozy up on the couch in the center of the main dining room.

After dinner, head for the Sirocco Lounge in the Wyndham's Casablanca Casino. Sip a cocktail and listen to live jazz (Thursdays through Saturdays). Or be daring and puff on an authentic Arabian hookah pipe. Later, pick a random number on the roulette wheel at the Sonesta's Crystal Casino. If that one's not a winner, try numbers that have special meaning for you, like each other's birthday, your wedding anniversary, or the day you met. End the evening with a walk—hand in hand of course—along the beach.

A PERFECT ALL-NIGHTER

Want to take advantage of everything Aruba has to offer? Here's an action-packed guide of things to do from sundown to sun-up.

Check out the Sunset Salute, accompanied by live music, at the Radisson Sunset Bar in the Radisson Aruba Caribbean Resort. Stick around for drink specials and merengue lessons.

Make dinner reservations at L'Escale, an upscale eatery overlooking the marina at the Aruba Sonesta Resort. You'll be serenaded by a Hungarian string trio as the courteous staff caters to your every need. The succulent dishes—fresh mahimahi, Caribbean-style snapper, rich chocolate soufflé—will surely satisfy your appetite.

At 9 PM, check out *Let's Go Latin*—an entertaining revue of singing and dancing—at the Sonesta Hotel's Stardust Theatre. Afterward, head to the trendy Garufa lounge for live jazz, a cognac, and perhaps a stogie. The chic bar stools are so comfortable, you may not want to leave. And besides, the later you get to the E Zone for dancing, the more fun you'll have.

Known for wild parties in its VIP room and for its eclectic collection of music (played 'til the wee hours), this is one place not to miss on your all-night adventure.

By sunrise, you should be on the beach—any beach. Afterward sip coffee, scan the local papers, and people-watch over breakfast at the Coco Plum café. Carbo-load for the new day with a *pastechi*—a potato-filled pastry.

The restaurant, typically packed with tourists, is now full of locals on an afternoon outing. They're joined at the bar by a visitor from New York who has befriended them to learn more about island life. After a few Balashi beers, the stories flow—tales of "yesterday's soup" (a belief that soup tastes better the second day) and jouvert (a street party that starts at 3 AM and lasts until sunrise to kick off Carnival). When their table is ready, the Arubans invite their new friend along to sample native specialties. The New Yorker hadn't planned to dine on goat stew, but when in Rome . . .

In This Chapter

eating out

THERE ARE A FEW HUNDRED RESTAURANTS ON ARUBA, including hotel establishments, neighborhood favorites, snack bars, and fast-food chains, so you're bound to find something to tantalize your taste buds. Thanks to the island's eclectic blend of cultures, local eateries serve the full gamut from Aruban food to American, Italian, French, Argentine, Asian, and Cuban. Chefs have to be creative here, since there's a limited number of locally grown ingredients—*maripampoen* (a vegetable that's often stewed with meat and potatoes), *hierba di hole* (a sweet-spicy herb used in fish soup), and *shimarucu* (a fruit similar to the cherry) are among the few.

Although most resorts offer better-than-average dining, don't be afraid to try one of the many excellent, reasonably priced, independent places. Ask locals about their favorite spots; some of the lesser-known restaurants offer food that's definitely worth sampling.

Most restaurants are along Palm Beach or in Oranjestad, easily accessible by taxi or the buses that run regularly to and from town. Some restaurants in Savaneta and San Nicolas are definitely worth the trip; a car is the best way to get there.

To give visitors a chance to sample the island's eclectic cuisine, the **ARUBA GASTRONOMIC ASSOCIATION** (Rooi Santo 21, Noord, tel. 297/8–62161; 800/477–2896 in the U.S., www.arubadining.com) has created a dine-around program involving several island restaurants. Here's how it works: you can buy tickets for 3 dinners ($109 per person), 5 dinners ($177), 7 dinners ($245), or 10 dinners ($339). Meals include an appetizer, an entrée, dessert, coffee or tea, and service charge (where applicable). Other programs, such as multicourse VIP gourmet dinners and after-dinner-show packages, are also available. You can buy dine-around tickets on the AGA's Web site (using an on-line order form), through travel agents, or at the De Palm Tours sales desk in your hotel.

PRICES AND DRESS

Aruba's elegant restaurants—where you might have to dress up a little (jackets for men, sundresses for women)—can be pricey. If you want to spend fewer florins, opt for the more casual spots, where being comfortable is the only dress requirement. A sweater draped over your shoulders will go a long way against the chill of air-conditioning. If you plan to eat in the open air, bring along insect repellent in case the mosquitoes get unruly.

CATEGORY	COST*
$$$	over $25
$$	$15–$25
$	under $15

*per person for a main course at dinner, excluding service charges or taxes.

HOW AND WHEN

To ensure you get to eat at the restaurants of your choice, make some calls when you get to the island—especially during high season—to secure reservations. If you're heading to a restaurant in Oranjestad for dinner, leave about 15 minutes earlier than you think you should; in-town traffic can become ugly once beach hours are over. Note that on Sunday you may have a hard time finding a restaurant that's open for lunch, and many eateries are closed for dinner on Sunday or Monday. Breakfast lovers are in luck. For quantity, check out the buffets at the Hyatt, Marriott, or Wyndham resorts or local joints like DeliFrance or Coco Plum.

Chowing Down Aruban Style

The finest restaurants require at the most only a jacket for men and a sundress for women. Still, after a day on the beach, even this might feel formal. For a truly casual bite, visit one of Aruba's ice cream trucks or frietjes (pushcarts) for inexpensive, authentic Aruban finger food. Two worth the trip are El Rey Snack Truck near the Seaport Cinemas in Oranjestad, for freshly fried chicken, pork chops, and fries, and The Cellar Frietje in Oranjestad's Seaport Village Marketplace, for the best saté in town. Other island delicacies include the following:

BITTERBALLEN: steaming, bite-size meatballs. The long versions are served with mustard and called kroket. Locals wash both varieties down with beer.

FREKEDEL: a shredded fish dipped in egg and bread crumbs, rolled into balls, and deep fried.

FRIET OR BATATA: french fries—served in paper cones or Styrofoam cups—that can be topped with ketchup; mayo; curry, peanut, or hot sauce; onions; and more.

KESHI YENA: a baked concoction of Gouda cheese, spices, and meat or seafood in a rich brown sauce.

NASIBAL: a lump of seasoned rice in a crunchy coating.

PAN BATI: a pancake made of cornmeal flour, sugar, salt, and baking powder; eaten with meat, fish, or soup.

PASTECHI: deep-fried meat, cheese, potato, or seafood-filled turnovers, popular for breakfast. Smaller versions are called empanas.

RASPAO: a paper cup full of shaved ice that's drenched in tamarind, guava, or passion fruit syrup.

ROTI: chicken, seafood, or vegetable curry in a tortilla-like wrap.

SATÉ: marinated chunks of chicken or pork on a bamboo skewer, grilled and served with spicy peanut sauce.

TOSTI: the ultimate grilled-cheese sandwich, often made with ham and pineapple or pepperoni.

California Pt.

32

Mt. Altovista

Bushiribana

1 A/B

2 A/B

Palm Beach

26 – 31

3 A/B

19 24

Noord

17 18

Tanki Leedert

4 A/B

Paradera

25

6 A/B

Eagle Beach

13 14 15

16

J.E. Irausquin Blvd.

Manchebo Beach

1 – 12

7 A/B

Santa Cruz

L. G. Smith Blvd.

Druif Bay

Oranjestad

1 A/B

Ba

N

0		4 miles
0		6 km

Amazonia Churrascaria, **20**

Bread Boutique, **14**

Brisas Del Mar, **36**

Buccaneer, **29**

Captain's Table, **17**

Charlie's Restaurant & Bar, **33**

Chez Mathilde, **2**

Coco Plum, **7**

Cuba's Cookin', **11**

Cyber Café, **10**

DeliFrance, **15**

Driftwood, **6**

Le Dôme, **18**

L'Escale, **1**

Flying Fishbone, **34**

French Steakhouse, **16**

Gasparito Restaurant & Art Gallery, **30**

El Gaucho Argentine Grill, **8**

Hostaria Da'Vittorio, **19**

Jakarta, **9**

Kowloon, **5**

Laguna, **23**

Madame Janette's, **31**

Old Cunucu House Restaurant, **25**

Paparazzi, **3, 24**

Papiamento, **27**

Pasion, **26**

El Patio, **13**

The Promenade, **35**

Que Pasa, **12**

Rigoletto, **28**

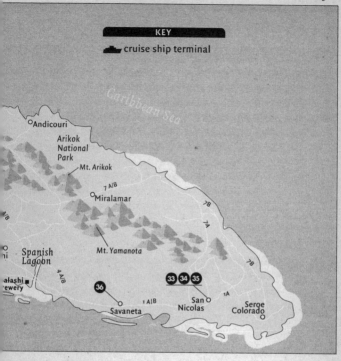

KEY

cruise ship terminal

Caribbean Sea

Andicouri

Arikok National Park

Mt. Arikok

7 A|B

Miralamar

7B

7A

Mt. Yamanota

7B

Spanish Lagoon

4 A|B

A|B

oni

alashi ewery

33 34 35

36

1A

1 A|B

San Nicolas

Serge Colorado

Savaneta

Argentine

$$–$$$ EL GAUCHO ARGENTINE GRILL. Faux-leather-bound books, tulip-top lamps, wooden chairs, and tile floors decorate this Argentine steak house, which has been in business for more than 20 years. A bottle of rich red wine from the extensive cellar and the melt-in-your-mouth garlic bread will tantalize your taste buds as you await your meal. Main dishes include thick *churrasco* (Argentine steak) smothered in peppers and onions and served with corn on the cob, potatoes, and broccoli, as well as the catch of the day served with salad, rice, broccoli, and fried plantains. For dessert, go for the *helado argentino* (vanilla ice cream with sweet-potato marmalade and caramel) or the *torta de queso*, otherwise known as cheesecake. *Wilhelminastraat 80, Oranjestad, tel. 297/8–23677. AE, D, MC, V. Closed Sun.*

Asian

$$–$$$ JAKARTA. The abundant use of flavorful Indonesian spices brings this restaurant to life. The signature rijsttafel, which consists of 20 miniature meat, fish, vegetable, and fruit dishes, jumps off the page of the straw-faced, banana-leaf-covered menu. Another popular choice is Indonesian-style chicken soup, made with bean sprouts, hard-boiled eggs, and chicken liver. Vegetarians can order egg rolls, vegetable soup, or meat-free rijsttafel. Sample the java juice (blue Curaçao, vodka, Cointreau, banana liqueur, and orange and pineapple juice) at the bamboo bar on the back patio amid wind chimes, big clay pots, and tiki torches (if the bugs bite, request a mosquito-repelling candle). *Wilhelminastraat 64, Oranjestad, tel. 297/8–38737. AE, D, DC, MC, V. Closed Tues.*

$–$$ KOWLOON. In addition to many Chinese provinces, Indonesia is also represented on the menu here. Try the *bami goreng*, a noodle dish with shreds of shrimp, pork, vegetables, and an intoxicating blend of herbs and spices. *Saté* (grilled strips of beef or chicken in a spicy peanut sauce), an assortment of curries, and steak prepared in a variety of ways are also available. The modern Asian decor blends well with the island's palms and sands. *Emmastraat 11, Oranjestad, tel. 297/8–24950. AE, MC, V.*

Café

$ **CYBER CAFÉ.** Vacations are great, but sometimes you still need contact with the outside world. Instead of toting your laptop through customs, click on at some of the kiosks in the lobbies of the major hotels. Or come to this café, where you can sip coffee as you surf ($5 for 35 minutes). Order some cake and pick up a cool cyber-surfing T-shirt ($12–$14) or a souvenir mouse-pad ($6) on your way out. *Royal Plaza Mall, L. G. Smith Blvd. 204, Oranjestad, tel. 297/8–24500. D, DC, MC, V.*

Caribbean

$–$$ **DRIFTWOOD.** Charming owner Francine Merryweather greets you at the door of this Aruban restaurant, which resembles a series of fishermen's huts. Her co-owner is likely out—personally reeling in your dinner. Order his catch prepared as you like (Aruban style—pan-fried with a fresh tomato, vegetable, and local herb sauce—is best) or another of the fine fish dishes. You can't go wrong with the white sangria punch; the maître d' may even let you take home the recipe. This restaurant participates in the AGA's dine-around program. *Klipstraat 12, Oranjestad, tel. 297/8–32515. MC, V. Closed Tues.*

$$–$$$ **GASPARITO RESTAURANT & ART GALLERY.** You'll find this
★ enchanting hideaway in a *cunucu* (country house) in Noord, not far from the hotels. The works of local artists' works are showcased on its softly lit walls. The Aruban specialties—pan bati, keshi yena, fish croquettes, conch stew—are feasts for the eye as well as the palate. The standout dish is the Gasparito chicken; the sauce was passed down from the owner's ancestors and features seven special ingredients including brandy, white wine, and pineapple juice. (The rest, they say, are secret.) The service is excellent. The restaurant participates in the AGA's dine-around program. *Gasparito 3, Noord, tel. 297/8–67044. AE, D, MC, V. Closed Sun. No lunch.*

$$–$$$ **OLD CUNUCU HOUSE RESTAURANT.** For more than seven years executive chef Ligia Maria has delighted diners with delicious

Some Like It Hot!

Arubans like their food spicy, and that's where the island's famous Madame Janette sauce comes in handy. It's made with chili peppers that are so hot they can burn your skin when they're broken open. Whether they're turned into pika, a relish-like mixture made with papaya, or sliced thin into vinegar and onions, these peppers are sure to set your mouth ablaze. Throw even a modest amount of Madame Janette sauce into a huge pot of soup and your taste buds will tingle. (Referring to the sauce's spicy nature, Aruban men often refer to an attractive woman as a "Madame Janette.") To tame the flames, don't go for a glass of water, as capsaicin, the compound in peppers that produces the heat, isn't water-soluble. Yogurt, sweet fruits, and starchy foods such as rice and bread are the best remedies.

homemade meals, securing her reputation as one of Aruba's finest chefs. Try the keshi yena or the broiled Caribbean lobster tail with thermidor cream sauce and Parmesan cheese topping. For dessert, indulge in Spanish coffee with Tia Maria and brandy. Saturday night you can have all the fajitas you can eat. This restaurant participates in the AGA's dine-around program. *Palm Beach 150, Noord, tel. 297/8–61666. AE, D, MC, V. No lunch.*

$$–$$$ **BRISAS DEL MAR.** A meal at this friendly place overlooking the
★ sea (and bus-accessible from hotels) is like dining in a private home. Old family recipes use such indigenous ingredients as the aromatic yerbiholé leaf (with a minty basil flavor). Try the steamy fish soup, keri keri (shredded fish kissed with annatto), or some of the island's best pan bati. The catch of the day cooked Aruban-style (panfried and covered with creole sauce, or in garlic butter

on request) has drawn a crowd for over 20 years. Reserve early for sunset gazing on the breezy terrace. This restaurant participates in the AGA's dine-around program. *Savaneta 222A, Savaneta, tel. 297/8–47718. AE, D, MC, V. Closed Monday.*

$ EL PATIO. For fast, cheap eats almost round-the-clock (they're open 23 hours a day), head for this roadside rest stop. Order at the counter and a waitress will bring your food to one of the plastic tables. The creole fish fillets, chicken wings, tenderloin sandwiches, and other items all come with fries, salad, and rice and beans. After your meal, order some *quesillo* (ice cream) and shoot a game of billiards in the back. *Sun Plaza Mall, L. G. Smith Blvd. 160, Oranjestad, tel. 297/8–34468. No credit cards.*

Contemporary

$$–$$$ L'ESCALE. You're missing out if you don't have at least one meal in this upscale eatery, rated the island's best restaurant in 2001. Sip wine as you gaze over bustling L. G. Smith Boulevard and watch the cruise ships depart. Start with the sautéed baby snails, then move on to Caribbean-style walnut-crusted snapper. For dessert try the rich chocolate soufflé. Sparkles and streamers decorate your table for special occasions, and the extensive cigar list can turn any night into a celebration. If time is short, opt for the pre-theater menu. *Aruba Sonesta Resort, L. G. Smith Blvd. 82, Oranjestad, tel. 297/8–36000. Reservations essential. AE, D, MC, V. No lunch.*

$$–$$$ PASION. You can satisfy your passions for food, drink, art, and culture at this hot spot. Enjoy the meals cooked up by the Venezuelan chef as you gaze at the colorful wall hangings and fine furnishings (and even take them home, for a price). Any of the tables is intimate, but large parties will feel most at home at the communal table in the wooden wine cellar. The sommalier decorks with finesse as you choose from a full list of tapas. Pop in on a wine-dinner night to sample the latest grapes. *Palm Beach Road, Noord, tel. 297/8–64752. Reservations essential. AE, D, MC, V. No lunch.*

Continental

$$$ CHEZ MATHILDE. ★ This elegant restaurant occupies one of Aruba's last surviving 19th-century houses. Ask to sit in the greenhouse atrium, which some say has the ambience of Paris. The outstanding French-style menu is constantly re-created by the Dutch chef, who has a deft touch with sauces. Feast on baked escargots, roasted breast of duck with tamarind sauce, ostrich fillet, or quail stuffed with calf's sweetbreads in a bell pepper sauce. Crêpes suzette and chocolate layer cake with *ponche crema* (Venezuelan brandied eggnog) sauce will win you over as you listen to the tinkling ivories. *Havenstraat 23, Oranjestad, tel. 297/8–34968. Reservations essential. AE, DC, MC, V. No lunch Sun.*

$$$ RUINAS DEL MAR. Surrounded by lush landscaping and waterfalls, the "Ruins of the Sea" is the perfect spot for a romantic dinner—whether indoors or on the waterfront patio. Exquisite Continental dishes are often given a Caribbean twist. Starters include jerk-spice carpaccio with mustard sauce, peppers, and Parmesan cheese and crab cakes with habanero hollandaise and Caribbean rémoulade. Seafood mixed grill and veal chop in a fig marsala sauce are among the favored entrées. Sunday brunch buffet comes complete with champagne. A 15% service charge is automatically added to your check. *Hyatt Regency Aruba Beach Resort & Casino, J. E. Irausquin Blvd. 85, Palm Beach, tel. 297/8–61234. AE, D, DC, MC, V. No lunch.*

$$–$$$ LE DÔME. ★ Belgian Peter Ballière and his partners imported 11,000 bricks from Antwerp to authenticate the Continental interior of this fine dining spot. The service is polished, the decor is sumptuous, and a local harpist and guitarist add considerable ambience. The Belgian endive soup is delicious; the tournedos Rossini (prime-cut beef in a port sauce accompanied by a goose-liver mousse), downright decadent. A seven-course set menu is also available. Try one of the eight imported Belgian beers or one of the wine list's 65 varieties. Savor champagne and a cup of coffee with the prix-fixe Sunday brunch. Change for dinner, as shorts are a no-no. *J. E. Irausquin Blvd. 224, Eagle Beach, tel. 297/8–71517. Reservations essential. AE, D, DC, MC, V. Closed Mon. and Sept.*

$$–$$$ **THE PROMENADE.** At this upscale spot (it's Aruba's only restaurant with valet parking) you and your significant other can try such appetizers as the crabmeat cocktail, the smoked salmon, or the escargots. Entrées like the filet mignon, T-bone steak, and the fresh catch of the day are prepared to your liking. It's the perfect end to a day spent exploring San Nicolas. *Zeppenfeldstraat 15, San Nicolas, tel. 297/8–43131. AE, D, DC, MC, V. Closed Mon.*

Cuban

$$–$$$ **CUBA'S COOKIN'.** Locals (restaurateurs among them) agree that the food here is "authentic-ethnic." When you enter this old *cunucu* (country) house, head straight for the bar to order a *mojito* (light rum, sugar, mint, and soda). Afterward you can unwind in the art-filled dining room before digging into your truly Cuban dish. *Wilhelminastraat 27, Oranjestad, tel. 297/8–80627. AE, MC, V.*

Eclectic

$$–$$$ **CAPTAIN'S TABLE.** If there were an award for the island's most improved restaurant, the Captain's Table—a participant in the AGA's dine-around program—would be a strong contender. After asking the resort's time-share owners for their input, food and beverage director Jerry Mans upgraded the menu, assembled a top-flight staff, and added nightly piano music. The cuisine is truly eclectic: some French, a little Italian, and a few others thrown in as well. The nautical surroundings might prompt you to try the *chopino*, an assortment of Italian seafood dishes with pastas and garlic bread. *La Cabana All Suite Beach Resort & Casino, J. E. Irausquin Blvd. 250, Eagle Beach, tel. 297/8–79000. AE, D, DC, MC, V.*

$$–$$$ **LAGUNA.** Louvered plantation-style doors frame the view at this colorful restaurant. You can dine inside in air-cooled comfort or outside on the terrace overlooking the lagoon. Enjoy local specialties, the Indo-Caribbean stir-fry, or a myriad of seafood options and an extensive sushi menu. Breakfast (either buffet or à la carte) is also a possibility. The restaurant participates in the

AGA dine-around program. J. E. Irausquin Blvd. 81, Palm Beach, tel. 297/8–66555. AE, D, DC, MC, V. No lunch.

$$–$$$ PAPIAMENTO. Longtime restaurateurs Lenie and Eduardo Ellis
★ converted their 130-year-old home into a bistro with an atmosphere that is elegant, intimate, and always romantic. You can feast sumptuously indoors surrounded by antiques or outdoors in a patio garden. The chefs mix Continental and Caribbean cuisines to produce favorites that include seafood and meat dishes. You can't go wrong by sharing the "clay pot" seafood medley for two. *Washington 61, Noord, tel. 297/8–64544. Reservations essential. AE, D, MC, V. No lunch. Closed Mon.*

$$–$$$ QUE PASA. A sign on the wall at the bar welcomes you with a friendly WHAT'S HAPPENING? in several languages. Before grabbing a table, select a glass of wine from the list wrapped around a bottle set on the bar and check out the local paintings on the walls. (You might even find one to bring home). Specialties include lobster bisque, rib-eye steaks with shiitake mustard sauce, and raspberry pie. The amiable ambience on the terrace may prompt you to hang out after dinner and trade stories with the people at the next table. *Wilhelminastraat 2, Oranjestad, tel. 297/8–34888. MC, V. No lunch.*

$$–$$$ VENTANAS DEL MAR. Floor-to-ceiling windows provide an ample view across a golf course and beyond to rolling sand dunes and the sea off the island's western tip. Dining on the intimate terrace amid flickering candles inspires romance. Sandwiches, salads, conch fritters, nachos, and quesadillas fill the midday menu; at night the emphasis is on seafood and meat. Sea bass in orange sauce and crab and corn chowder are specialties. This restaurant participates in the AGA dine-around program. *Tierra del Sol Golf Course, Malmokweg, tel. 297/8–67800. AE, D, DC, MC, V. Closed Mon. Apr.–Nov.*

$–$$ BUCCANEER. Imagine you're in a sunken ship where sharks, barracudas, and groupers swim past the portholes. That's what you'll find at Buccaneer, a restaurant with a fantastic 7,500-gallon saltwater aquarium. The chefs prepare surf-and-turf fare with European élan. Head to this old stone building flanked by heavy black chains early (around 5:45 PM) to snag a booth beside the aquarium and order the catch of the day, shrimp with Pernod, or smoked pork cutlets with sausage, sauerkraut, and potatoes. The restaurant participates in the AGA dine-around program. *Gasparito 11-C, Noord, tel. 297/8–66172. AE, MC, V. No lunch. Closed Sun.*

$–$$ CHARLIE'S RESTAURANT & BAR. Charlie's has been a San Nicolas hangout for more than 50 years. The walls and ceiling are *covered* with license plates, hard hats, sombreros, life preservers, baseball pennants, intimate apparel—you name it. The draw here is the nonstop party atmosphere—somewhere between a frat house and a beach bar. Decent but somewhat overpriced specialties are tenderloin and "shrimps jumbo and dumbo" (dumb because they were caught). And don't leave before sampling Charlie's "honeymoon sauce" (so called because it's really hot). *Zeppenfeldstraat 56, San Nicolas, tel. 297/8–45086. AE, D, MC, V. Closed Sun.*

$–$$ COCO PLUM. Grab a *pastechi* (meat-, cheese-, or seafood-filled turnover) and go, or stick around to relax under thatch-roof huts and watch life unfold along Caya Betico Croes. Locals meet here for ham or tuna sandwiches, red snapper platters, and chicken wings. Slake your thirst with an all-natural fruit drink in flavors like watermelon, lemon, papaya, tamarind, and passion fruit. At the counter, order *loempias* (egg rolls stuffed with vegetables, chicken, or shrimp) or *empanas* (stuffed pockets of corn meal). *Caya Betico Croes 100, Oranjestad, tel. 297/8–31176. AE, MC, V. No dinner. Closed Sun.*

$–$$ DELIFRANCE. If you're eager to skip the traditional hour-long hotel
★ breakfast, DeliFrance offers the perfect solution—yummy, freshly baked baguettes and croissants. Try the All-American Breakfast Combo (toast, scrambled eggs, bacon, coffee, and fresh orange juice). Don't leave without tasting the Beukenhorst Koffie, a

Yo, Ho, Ho and a Cake of Rum

When Venancio Felipe Bareno came to Aruba from Spain 50 years ago, little did he know that his family's rum cake recipe would make culinary history. Now the sweet little desert is known around the world. His nephew, Bright Bakery owner Franklin Bareno, packages the pastry for local and international sales. The history of this island favorite is printed on the side of the box. Made with Aruban Palmeira rum, Natural Bridge Aruba's rum cake makes the perfect gift for folks back home. Available in two sizes, the vacuum-sealed cakes stay fresh for up to six months. The company is registered in the United States, so you can transport the cakes through customs. At press time, a lower-calorie version was slated to be on the market soon.

brand of Costa Rican coffee, and the *poffertjes* (miniature Dutch pancakes topped with melted butter and powdered sugar). For lunch there are salads, sandwiches, and, of course, pastries. The kids can play outside while you flip through American and European magazines. *Certified Mega Mall, L. G. Smith Blvd. 150, Oranjestad, tel. 297/8–86006. AE, D, MC, V. No dinner.*

$ **BREAD BOUTIQUE.** Office workers regularly stop by this tiny bread shop for their morning coffee, a bagel, or banana-nut bread. For lunch on-the-go, enjoy pumpkin soup, sugar- and sodium-free breads, crab salad, chicken saté, turkey salad, or fresh fruit. Grab one of the window seats for some people-watching while you eat, or take your food with you. *Sun Plaza Mall, L. G. Smith Blvd. 160, Oranjestad, tel. 297/8–80503. No credit cards. No dinner. Closed weekends.*

French

$$–$$$ **MADAME JANETTE'S.** The candles set around the outdoor garden
★ and the Caribbean-influenced European menu have set romantics
abuzz about this eatery between Palm Beach and Eagle Beach.
Start with creamy Hollandaise and Béarnaise dressed shellfish,
sirloin, or lamb, or try the pizza topped with salmon tartare and
goat cheese. Crème brûlée or stuffed crepes finish your fine meal.
If you're in the mood for something lighter, there are tasty salads,
grilled fish, and lower-fat tenderloins. The restaurant participates
in the AGA dine-around program. *Cunucu Abao 37, Cunucu Abao, tel.
297/8–70184. AE, MC, V. Closed Tues. No lunch.*

Italian

$$–$$$ **HOSTARIA DA' VITTORIO.** Part of the fun at this family-oriented
lunch and dinner spot is watching chef Vittorio Muscariello
prepare regional specialties in the open kitchen. Rising above the
decibel level of the crowd, the staff helps you choose wines from
the extensive list and recommends portions of hot and cold
antipasti, risottos, and pastas. Try the *branzino al sale* (sea bass baked
in a hard salt shell). Exciting presentations and warm service
reflect the management's stated desire to honor the essence of
Italy: "ancient, but always young." As you leave, pick up some
limoncello liqueur or olive oil at the door. A 15% gratuity is
automatically added to your bill. *L. G. Smith Blvd. 380, Palm Beach,
tel. 297/8–63838. AE, MC, V.*

$$–$$$ **RIGOLETTO.** Owner Tino Nicita mastered the art of cooking in his
native Taormina, and diners have enjoyed generous portions of
his authentic Italian dishes for more than 10 years. Start with the
antipasto of salami, prosciutto, and cheese or the calamari rings
with marinara. Then move on to the *capellini* (angel hair pasta)
sautéed in olive oil with shrimp and bay scallops or the ziti with
diced lobster, vodka, tomato sauce, and a touch of heavy cream.
Save room for the cannoli. *Bubali 16, Noord, tel. 297/8–37733. AE,
MC, V. Closed Mon.*

Weight Conversion Chart

KILOGRAMS/POUNDS

To change kilograms (kg) to pounds (lb), multiply kg by 2.20.

To change lb to kg, multiply lb by .455.

KG TO LB	LB TO KG
1=2.2	1=.45
2=4.4	2=.91
3=6.6	3=1.4
4=8.8	4=1.8
5=11.0	5=2.3
6=13.2	6=2.7
7=15.4	7=3.2
8=17.6	8=3.6

GRAMS/OUNCES

To change grams (g) to ounces (oz), multiply g by .035.

To change oz to g, multiply oz by 28.4.

G TO OZ	OZ TO G
1=.04	1=28
2=.07	2=57
3=.11	3=85
4=.14	4=114
5=.18	5=142
6=.21	6=170
7=.25	7=199
8=.28	8=227

$$–$$$ TUSCANY. Two chefs at this casually elegant restaurant won awards in the Caribbean Culinary Competition, and when you sample the food you'll know why. The *spannochie prima donna con capellini d'angelo* (sautéed shrimp with prosciutto, shallots, wild mushrooms, and artichokes in a light grappa cream sauce on angel hair pasta) is a delight. Don't despair if the extensive menu doesn't feature your particular fancy—the kitchen may be up for a challenge. The personalized service, excellent wine list, and soft piano music make for a special evening. *Aruba Marriott Resort & Stellaris Casino, L. G. Smith Blvd. 101, Palm Beach, tel. 297/8–69000. Reservations essential. AE, DC, MC, V. No lunch.*

$–$$ PAPARAZZI. The savvy owners of Chez Mathilde have put their fingers into more than one pie—they now have a pair of gourmet pizza restaurants. Both places are colorfully decorated and adorned with tropical greenery. Choose from hearty pastas and vegetarian or seafood pies—all with thin, crispy crusts. There's even apple pizza (topped with a scoop of vanilla ice cream) for dessert. Take in the mellow music from your outdoor table at the location in Allegro Plaza. Paparazzi participates in the AGA dine-around program. *Seaport Village Marketplace, L. G. Smith Blvd. 9, Oranjestad, tel. 297/8–35966; Allegro Plaza Mall, J. E. Irausquin Blvd. 368, Palm Beach, tel. 297/8–63659. AE, D, DC, MC, V. No lunch.*

Seafood

$$–$$$ FLYING FISHBONE. This restaurant is a little hard to find, but it's
★ worth the effort for a relaxing beachfront meal. The Middle Eastern decor transports you back to the days of *Casablanca* as soon as you walk through the door. Reserve a spot on the wooden deck that faces the beach or dig your toes into the sand at a table on the water's edge. Tuna, grouper, and other fresh catches are creatively prepared and artistically presented. Appetizers and desserts are truly tasty. *Savaneta 344, San Nicolas, tel. 297/8–42506. AE, D, DC, MC, V. Closed Sun.*

$$–$$$ WATERFRONT CRABHOUSE. If you flew to Aruba on American Airlines, there was probably a 3,000-pound container of seafood in the belly of the plane. The Waterfront Crabhouse receives a delivery of live Maine lobsters each day, to stock its lobster tank—the largest in the Caribbean. Herb and Parmesan-encrusted shrimp, served with marmalade and horseradish sauce, is sautéed on a lava-rock gas grill that sears the exteriors while leaving their centers juicy. A burger or sandwich makes a tasty lunch. The restaurant participates in the AGA dine-around program. *Seaport Village Marketplace, L. G. Smith Blvd. 9, Oranjestad, tel. 297/8–35858 or 297/8–36767. AE, D, DC, MC, V.*

Steak

$$–$$$ AMAZONIA CHURRASCARIA. The cozy surroundings and festive atmosphere will reel you in, but this Brazilian steakhouse offers much more. Charcoal-grilled meats are expertly prepared and charismatically carved right at your table, and the comprehensive salad bar includes items you didn't even know existed. You can opt for unique appetizers and desserts like fried plantains and flan. Eat to your heart's content—it's all for a fixed price. *J. E. Irausquin Blvd. 374, Palm Beach, tel. 297/8–64444. AE, DC, MC, V. No lunch. Closed Mon.*

$$–$$$ FRENCH STEAKHOUSE. You can hear someone say "ooh-la-la" whenever a delectable steak is set on some lucky diner's plate at this well-known restaurant. People come here from all over the island, which means the lines are often out the door. Classical music plays in the background as the friendly staff serves hearty meat entrées, fresh tuna or grouper, and vegetable dishes. A five-course dinner includes a bottle of wine for a nice price. The eatery is a participant in the AGA's dine-around program. *Manchebo Beach Resort, J. E. Irausquin Blvd. 55, Eagle Beach, tel. 297/8–23444. AE, DC, MC, V. No lunch.*

The Goods on Gouda

Each year Holland exports more than 250,000 tons of cheese to more than 100 countries, and Gouda (pronounced how-da) is one of the most popular. Gouda, named for the city where it's produced, travels well and gets harder, saltier, and more flavorful as it ages. According to Patrick Paris, purchasing director of Consales Aruba, a Gouda wholesaler that sells about 330,000 pounds of cheese each year, there are six types of Gouda: young (at least 4 weeks old), semi-major (8 weeks old), major (4 months old), ultra-major (7 months old), old (10 months old), and vintage (more than a year old). When buying cheese, look for the control seal that confirms the name of the cheese, its country of origin, its fat content, and that it was officially inspected.

It was late in the day when the cruise ship docked. An agitated couple dashed into a jewelry shop and rushed to the gem counter, their shopping clock ticking. "Is anything wrong?" asked the clerk. "Well," said the woman, "our ship was delayed, and now we don't have time to buy all the things we wanted: earrings for my mother, a sarong for my sister, linens for our daughter, and a sculpture for our son." To accommodate the couple—and the 3,000 other passengers—the ship extended its stay until midnight and most shops in town remained open.

In This Chapter

shopping

ARUBA'S SOUVENIR AND CRAFTS STORES ARE FULL of Dutch porcelains and figurines, as befits the island's heritage. Dutch cheese is a good buy (you're allowed to bring up to 10 pounds of hard cheese through U.S. customs), as are hand-embroidered linens and any products made from the native aloe vera plant—sunburn cream, face masks, skin refreshers. Local arts and crafts run toward wood carvings and earthenware emblazoned with ARUBA: ONE HAPPY ISLAND and the like.

"Duty free" is a magical term. In fact, about 30% of the island's annual cruise ship visitors teem into the many duty-free stores just steps from the terminal as soon as their ship docks. Most North Americans, who find clothing to be less expensive back home, buy perfume and jewelry; South Americans tend to shell out lots of cash on a variety of brand-name merchandise.

Island merchants are honest and pleasant. Still, if you encounter price markups, unsatisfactory service, or other shopping obstacles, call the tourist office, which will in turn contact the Aruba Merchants Association. A representative of the association will speak with the merchant on your behalf, even if the store isn't an association member.

HOW AND WHEN

It's easy to spend money on Aruba. Most stores accept American currency and Aruban florins (written as "Afl") as well as credit cards and traveler's checks. Since there's no sales tax, the price you see on the tag is what you pay. (Note that although large stores in town and at hotels are duty free, in tiny shops and studios you may have to pay the ABB, or value-added tax, of 6.5%.) Don't try to bargain in stores, where it's considered rude to haggle. At flea markets and souvenir stands, however, you might be able to strike a deal.

At press time, two proposals that affect shopping hours were under consideration: one would extend store hours to 8 PM at least once each month; the other would force shops to close on Sunday. For now, stores are open Monday through Saturday 8:30 or 9 to 6. Some stores stay open through the lunch hour (noon–2), and many open when cruise ships are in port on Sundays and holidays. The later you shop in downtown Oranjestad, the easier it will be to find a place to park. Also, later hours mean slightly lower temperatures. In fact, the Aruba Merchants Association is one force behind the effort to have shops stay open later so that visitors who like to spend the day on the beach can shop in the cool of the evening.

AREAS AND MALLS

Oranjestad's **CAYA G. F. BETICO CROES** is Aruba's chief shopping street, lined with several duty-free boutiques and jewelry stores noted for the aggressiveness of their vendors on cruise-ship days. Most malls are in Oranjestad and are attractive gabled, pastel-hued recreations of Dutch colonial architecture.

For late- night shopping, head to the **ALHAMBRA CASINO SHOPPING ARCADE** (L. G. Smith Blvd. 47, Manchebo Beach), open 5 PM–midnight. Souvenir shops, boutiques, and fast-food outlets fill the arcade, which is attached to the busy casino. Although small, the **AQUARIUS MALL** (Elleboogstraat 1, Oranjestad) has some upscale shops.

If you blink, you might miss the good finds at **DUTCH CROWN CENTER** (L. G. Smith Blvd. 150 [some shops face Havenstraat], Oranjestad), a tiny complex tucked between the major malls.

The **HOLLAND ARUBA MALL** (Havenstraat 6, Oranjestad) houses a collection of smart shops and eateries.

Stores at the **PORT OF CALL MARKETPLACE** (L. G. Smith Blvd. 17, Oranjestad) sell fine jewelry, perfumes, duty-free liquor, batiks, crystal, leather goods, and fashionable clothing. The **ROYAL PLAZA MALL** (L. G. Smith Blvd. 94, Oranjestad), across from the cruise-ship terminal, has cafés, a post office (open Monday–Friday, 8–3:30), and such stores as Nautica, Benetton, Tommy Hilfiger, and Gandelman Jewelers. This is where you'll find the Cyber Café, where you can send e-mail and get your caffeine fix all in one stop.

Five minutes from the cruise ship terminal, the **SEAPORT VILLAGE MALL** (L. G. Smith Blvd. 82, Oranjestad) is home to the Crystal Casino. More than 120 stores sell merchandise to meet every taste and budget. **STRADA I** and **STRADA II** (corner of Klipstraat and Rifstraat, Oranjestad) are shopping complexes in Dutch-style buildings painted in pastels.

SPECIALTY ITEMS

Cigars

You'll find cigars at **LA CASA DEL HABANO** (Royal Plaza Mall, L. G. Smith Blvd. 94, Oranjestad, tel. 297/8–38509). At the **CIGAR EMPORIUM** (Seaport Village Mall, L. G. Smith Blvd. 82, Oranjestad, tel. 297/8–25479), the Cubans come straight from the climate-controlled humidor. Choose from Cohiba, Montecristo, Romeo y Julieta, Partagas, and more. **SUPERIOR TOBACCO** (L. G. Smith Blvd. 120, Oranjestad, tel. 297/8–23220) is a good place to shop for stogies.

Clothes

Stop by the **ACTIVE BOUTIQUE** (Dutch Crown Center, Havenstraat 21, Oranjestad, tel. 297/8–37008) for SOS swimsuits made in Brazil. You can pick up a sexy, high-cut two-

Ronchi de Cuba's Aruban Style

"Shopping has recently become tremendously advanced on Aruba," says local fashion designer Ronchi de Cuba. "We're seeing higher-end fashion that's more reasonably priced, from companies like Fendi and Gucci, and the shopping area is still growing." He says the best time to get great buys at the high-end stores is in January, when the holidays are over and the racks are being cleared for the new season.

De Cuba became involved in fashion at age 17, thanks to a high school physical-education assignment where he taught a dance class and presented a show that incorporated theater, choreography, and fashion. After attending college in Miami, Florida, de Cuba returned to his native Aruba to work at a modeling agency. Soon after, he opened his own agency to promote local entertainment and style.

The first Ronchi de Cuba design was a haute-couture number created for Miss Aruba 1999; he has since gone on to create ready-to-wear swimwear, menswear, womenswear, and junior lines. When he's not cutting clothes, the designer travels to New York, Miami, and Paris to peek into the shops and showrooms of major designers.

De Cuba clothes are constructed of fabrics suitable for a warm climate: crepe linens, silk georgettes, and shantungs for day; brocade, wool crepe, crepe de chine, and silk chiffon for evening. Inspired by such designers as John Galliano, Dolce & Gabbana, and Prada, his collections feature playful color schemes that incorporate dark solids, brights, and prints. He turns out a spring-summer collection and a holiday-cruise collection each year and held his first show in the U.S. in 2000. Look for his label at stores in the Seaport Village Marketplace and the Royal Plaza Mall or at his own shop—Revolution—which is under E-Zone in Oranjestad.

piece for only $62. Even racier are the thongs and bikinis in tropical colors. Get creative here by mixing and matching.

At **AGATHA BOUTIQUE** (Seaport Village Mall, L. G. Smith Blvd. 82, Oranjestad, tel. 297/8–37965) splurge on some high-style outfits (some up to size 18), shoes, and bags by New York fashion designer Agatha Brown. Try at least one of her two signature fragrances, derived from floral and citrus scents. **MODA ACTUAL** (Caya G. F. Betico Croes 49, Oranjestad, tel. 297/8–31202) rotates its reasonably priced, high-quality merchandise about every two months. Popular items include preshrunk cotton tank tops and T-shirts for men and women.

People come to **CAPERUCITA RAJA** (Wilhelminastraat 17, Oranjestad, tel. 297/8–36166) for designer baby, children's, and junior clothes, as well as a wide selection of shoes. Outfits that cost $21 here sell for more than three times that amount at Saks Fifth Avenue. Forget to pack your intimates? **COLOMBIA MODA** (Wilhelminastraat 19, Oranjestad, tel. 297/8–23460) will help complete your wardrobe with lingerie made of high-quality microfiber fabrics. **CONFETTI** (Seaport Village Mall, L. G. Smith Blvd. 82, Oranjestad, tel. 297/8–38614) has the hottest European and American swimsuits, cover-ups, and other beach essentials.

EXTREME SPORTS (Royal Plaza Mall, L. G. Smith Blvd. 94, Oranjestad, tel. 297/8–38458) sells everything sportsaholics could ever need. Invest in a set of in-line skates or a boogie board or pick up a backpack, bathing suit, or pair of reef walkers in funky colors. **J. L. PENHA & SONS** (Caya G. F. Betico Croes 11/13, Oranjestad, tel. 297/8–24160 or 297/8–24161), a venerated name in Aruba, sells perfumes and cosmetics. It stocks such brands as Boucheron, Swiss Army, Dior, Cartier, and Givenchy.

At **MANGO** (Main St. 9, Oranjestad, tel. 297/8–29700)—part of an international chain—you'll find fashions from as far away as Spain. If the Aruban sun doesn't make your life sizzle, the sexy lingerie at **SECRETS OF ARUBA** (Seaport Village Mall, L. G. Smith

Blvd. 82, Oranjestad, tel. 297/8–30897) just might. The store also sells oils and lotions that aren't meant for getting a tan. As the many repeat customers will tell you, **SUN + SAND** (Dutch Crown Center, L. G. Smith Blvd. 150, Oranjestad, tel. 297/8–38812) is the place for T-shirts, sweatshirts, polo shirts, and cover-ups.

You'll find innovative active wear at the **TOMMY HILFIGER BOUTIQUE** (Royal Plaza Mall, L. G. Smith Blvd. 94, Oranjestad, tel. 297/8–38548). Be sure to check out the Tommy Jeans store as well. Menswear reigns supreme at **LA VENEZOLANA** (Steenweg 12, Oranjestad, tel. 297/8–21444). You'll find blazers and suits as well as jeans, belts, and shoes. Look for such names as Givenchy, Lee Jeans, and Van Heusen.

WULFSEN & WULFSEN (Caya G. F. Betico Croes 52, Oranjestad, tel. 297/8–23823) has been one of the most highly regarded men's and women's clothing stores in Aruba and the Netherlands Antilles for nearly 30 years. It carries elegant suits for men and linen cocktail dresses for women, and it's also a great place to buy bathing suits and Bermuda shorts.

Duty-Free Goods

For perfumes, cosmetics, men's and women's clothing, and leather goods (including Bally shoes), stop in at **ARUBA TRADING COMPANY** (Caya G. F. Betico Croes 12, Oranjestad, tel. 297/8–22602), which has been in business more than 70 years.

LITTLE SWITZERLAND (Caya G. F. Betico Croes 14, Oranjestad, tel. 297/8–21192; Royal Plaza Mall, L. G. Smith Blvd. 94, Oranjestad, tel. 297/8–34057), the St. Thomas–based giant, is the place to go for china, crystal, and fine tableware. You'll also find good buys on Omega and Rado watches, Swarovski and Baccarat crystal, and Lladro figurines.

At **WEITNAUER** (Caya G. F. Betico Croes 29, Oranjestad, tel. 297/8–22790) you'll find specialty Lenox items as well as a wide range of fragrances.

Food

The clean, orderly **KONG HING SUPERMARKET** (L. G. Smith Blvd. 152, Bushiri, tel. 297/8–25545) stocks all the comforts of home—from fresh cuts of meat to prepackaged salads to Lean Cuisine dinners. The liquor section offers everything from exotic liqueurs to beer. There's also a pharmacy with name-brand items like Goody hair supplies and Bausch & Lomb eye-care products. The market, which is open Monday to Saturday 8–8 and Sunday 9–1 accepts MasterCard, Visa, and Discover for purchases of $10 or more. There's an ATM on the premises.

The family-owned and -operated **LING & SONS SUPERMARKET** (Italiestraat 26, Eagle Beach, tel. 297/8–32370, www.visitaruba. com/ling&sons) is one of the island's top grocers. In addition to a wide variety of foods, there's a Dutch bakery, a deli, a butcher shop, and a well-stocked liquor store. If you plan ahead, the store can have a package of essential foodstuffs delivered to your hotel room in time for your arrival. The market is open Monday to Saturday 8–8 and Sunday 9–1. Before the December holidays, the store sometimes stays open an hour later on weekdays.

Gifts and Souvenirs

ART AND TRADITION HANDICRAFTS (Caya G. F. Betico Croes 30, Oranjestad, tel. 297/8–36534; Royal Plaza Mall, L. G. Smith Blvd. 94, Oranjestad, tel. 297/8–27862) sells intriguing items that look hand-painted. Buds from the *mopa mopa* tree are boiled to form a resin colored by vegetable dyes. Artists then stretch the resin by hand and mouth. Tiny pieces are cut and layered to form intricate designs—truly unusual gifts.

The **ARTISTIC BOUTIQUE** (Caya G. F. Betico Croes 25, Oranjestad, tel. 297/8–23142; Wyndham Aruba Beach Resort and Casino, J. E. Irausquin Blvd. 77, tel. 297/8–64466 ext. 3508; Seaport Village Mall, L. G. Smith Blvd. 82, Oranjestad, tel. 297/8–32567; Holiday Inn Aruba Beach Resort & Casino, J. E. Irausquin

Blvd. 230, tel. 297/8–33383) has been in business for 30 years. It's known for its Giuseppe Armani figurines from Italy, usually sold at a 20% discount; Aruban hand-embroidered linens; gold and silver jewelry; and porcelain and pottery from Spain.

EL BOHIO (Holiday Inn Aruba Beach Resort & Casino, Port of Call Marketplace, L. G. Smith Blvd. 17, Oranjestad, tel. 297/8–29178) will charm you with its wooden-hut displays holding Arawak-style pottery, Dutch shoes, and wind chimes. You'll also find classic leather handbags. **CREATIVE HANDS** (Socotorolaan 5, Oranjestad, tel. 297/8–35665) sells porcelain and ceramic miniatures of cunucu (country) houses and divi-divi trees, but the store's real draw is its exquisite Japanese dolls. For pottery lovers, **KWA KWA** (Port of Call Marketplace, L. G. Smith Blvd. 17, Oranjestad, tel. 297/8–39471) is a paradise. There are wind chimes, pottery, and knickknacks galore—all made of ceramic, of course. Other items include embroidered bags.

While you wait 30 minutes for your film to be developed at **NEW FACE PHOTO** (Dutch Crown Center, Havenstraat 27, Oranjestad, tel. 297/8–29510) you can shop for gifts. At **VIBES** (Royal Plaza Mall, L. G. Smith Blvd. 93, Oranjestad, tel. 297/8–37949) treat yourself to a Monte Crisco or Cohiba cigar. Clothes from Aruba and Indonesia, hand-painted mobiles, and bamboo wind chimes are among the goodies at **TROPICAL WAVE** (Port of Call, L. G. Smith Blvd. 17, Oranjestad, tel. 297/8–21905).

Housewares

Locals swear by **DECOR HOME FASHIONS** (Steenweg 14, Oranjestad, tel. 297/8–26620), which sells sheets, towels, place mats, and other linens imported from Italy, Germany, Holland, Portugal, and the United States.

Jewelry

In business for more than 25 years, **BOOLCHAND'S** (Seaport Village Mall, L. G. Smith Blvd. 82, Oranjestad, tel. 297/8–30147) sells jewelry and watches. It also fills its 6,000-square-ft space with leather goods, cameras, and electronics. If green fire is your passion, **COLOMBIAN EMERALDS** (Seaport Village Mall, L. G. Smith Blvd. 82, Oranjestad, tel. 297/8–36238) has a dazzling array. There's also a fine array of watches by Breitling, Baume & Mercier, Jaeger-Le Coultre, Ebel, Seiko, Citizen, and Tissot.

GANDELMAN JEWELERS (Royal Plaza Mall, L. G. Smith Blvd. 94, Oranjestad, tel. 297/8–34433) sells Gucci and Rolex watches at reasonable prices, as well as gold bracelets, and a full line of Lladro figurines. **KENRO JEWELERS** (Seaport Village Mall, L. G. Smith Blvd. 82, Oranjestad, tel. 297/8–34847 or 297/8–33171) has two stores in the same mall, attesting to the popularity of its stock of bracelets and necklaces from the Ramon Leopard collection; jewelry by Arando, Micheletto, and Blumei; and various brands of watches. There are also other six other locations, including some in the major hotels.

Leather Goods

ALIVIO (Steenweg 12-1, Oranjestad, no phone) has shoes for men, women, and children. Whether you're walking around town by day or dressing up for dinner by night, you'll find something suitable in this shop in Oranjestad. Look for Birkenstock from Germany, Piedro and Wolky from Holland, and Mephisto from France.

If you get lucky, you'll catch one of the year's big sales at **GUCCI** (Seaport Village Mall, L. G. Smith Blvd. 82, Oranjestad, tel. 297/8–33952), when prices are slashed on handbags, luggage, wallets, shoes, watches, belts, and ties. The store also offers 20% off various items throughout the year. Most days, though, don't expect bargains, as prices are comparable to those at the Gucci outlets back home. One of Oranjestad's most exciting openings is slated for the holiday shopping season of 2002, when **FERRAGAMO** is scheduled to open the doors of a brand new boutique behind Royal Plaza Mall.

Oblivious to the casino's din, a handful of blackjack players are on the edge of their seats. Each has split his or her cards, and there's a lot of money at stake. The dealer's hand totals 16. One player wipes the sweat from his brow; another takes a long drag on her cigarette and slowly exhales. A group of onlookers whisper their predictions. With a flourish, the dealer pulls his final card—a queen! The players shout for joy.

In This Chapter

casinos

THERE WAS A TIME WHEN WOMEN DRESSED in evening gowns and men donned suits for a chic, glamorous night in Aruba's casinos. In the mid-'80s, however, the Alhambra casino opened, touting its philosophy of "barefoot elegance." Suddenly shorts and T-shirts became acceptable attire. The relaxed dress code made gaming seem an affordable pastime rather than a luxury.

Aruba's casinos now attract high rollers, low-stakes betters, and non-gamblers alike. Games include slot machines, blackjack (both beloved by North Americans), baccarat (preferred by South Americans), craps, roulette—even betting on sports events. Theaters, restaurants, bars, and cigar shops have added another dimension to the casinos. Now you can go out for dinner, a show, after-dinner drinks, and gambling all under one roof. In between games, you can get to know other patrons and swap tips and tales. The many local entertainers who rotate among the casinos add to the excitement.

THE CASINOS

Except for the free-standing Alhambra, most casinos are found in hotels; all are on Palm Beach or Eagle Beach or in downtown Oranjestad. Although the minimum age to enter is 18, some venues are relaxed about this rule. By day, "barefoot elegance" is the norm in all casinos, although many establishments have a shirt-and-shoes requirement. Evening dress is expected to be more polished, though still casual. In high season, the casinos are open from just before noon to the wee hours; in low season (May to November), they may not start dealing until late afternoon.

If you plan to play large sums of money, check in with the casino upon arrival so that you'll be rewarded for your business. Most hotels offer gambling goodies—complimentary meals at local restaurants, chauffeured tours, and, in the cases of big winners, high-roller suites—for patrons spending a lot of cash. Even small-scale gamblers may be entitled to coupons for meals and discounted rooms.

ALLEGRO CASINO. Famous movie characters gaze down at you from a 30-ft mural as you take your chance at one of 245 slots or at blackjack, roulette, poker, craps, baccarat, and Caribbean stud poker tables. The casino at the Allegro Resort opens daily at noon for slots and at 5 PM for all other games. The entire gaming floor joins in the free full-card bingo game held nightly at 10:30. Anyone who scores a full card within the first 50 calls wins a clean grand; everyone who shows a full card after that walks away with $100. Friday at 8 PM sees a slot tournament, and look for double jackpots daily from 3 PM to 5 PM. You can hang around till 4 AM. *J. E. Irausquin Blvd. 83, Palm Beach, tel. 297/8–69039, www.allegroresorts.com.*

ALHAMBRA CASINO. Here, amid the Spanish-style arches and leaded glass, a "Moorish slave" named Roger gives every gambler a hearty handshake upon entering. The atmosphere is casual, and with $5 tables, no one need feel intimidated. Try your luck at blackjack, Caribbean stud poker, three-card poker, roulette, craps, or one of the 300 slot machines that accept American nickels, quarters, and dollars. Head to one of the novelty touch-screen machines, each of which has a variety of games. There's also bingo every Sunday, Monday, and Thursday beginning at 1 PM. If you fill your card, you can collect the grand prize of a few hundred dollars—not bad for a $5 investment. Be sure to sign up for the Alhambra Advantage Card, which gives you a point for each dollar you spend—even if you lose at the tables, you can still go home with prizes. Of course, winners can spend their earnings immediately at the many on-site shops. The casino is owned by the Divi Divi resorts, and golf carts run to and from nearby hotels every 15 minutes or so. The slots here open daily at 10 AM; gaming tables operate from 6 PM 'til 4 AM. L. G. Smith Blvd. 47, Oranjestad, tel. 297/8–35000 ext. 480/482.

CASABLANCA CASINO. Smart money is on the Wyndham Aruba Beach Resort's quietly elegant casino, which has a Humphrey Bogart theme and a tropical color scheme. Spend some time at the blackjack, roulette, craps, stud poker, and baccarat tables or the slot machines. Seek out the unique Feature Frenzy machines, which reportedly pay out $6,000 jackpots daily. If gambling isn't your style, venture into the Sirocco Lounge for exotic cocktails, authentic Arabian hookah pipes, and live jazz most nights at 9. Or you can take in the Aruba Carnival Havana Tropical shows. The casino is open daily from noon to 4 AM. J. E. Irausquin Blvd. 77, Palm Beach, tel. 297/8–64466, www.wyndham.com.

CENTURION CASINO. Real musical instruments decorate the walls of this small, homey establishment in the Aruba Grand Beach Resort. The clientele is flecked with lawyers and accountants fresh from the States. Like you, they've come to play blackjack, roulette, baccarat, craps, poker, and slots. Look for such theme nights as Lucky Joker Night, when the recipient of a secret joker stashed in a blackjack deck wins a cash prize. The casino opens at 10 AM for slots, noon for other games. The fun doesn't end until 2 AM. J. E. Irausquin Blvd. 79, Palm Beach, tel. 297/8–63900 ext. 149, www.arubagrand.com.

COPACABANA CASINO. Ablaze with neon, the Hyatt Regency Aruba Beach Resort's ultramodern casino is an enormous complex with a Carnival-in-Rio theme. The most popular games here are slots, blackjack, craps, and baccarat. Slots and some other games are available at noon, the dice start rolling at 6 PM, and all other pursuits are open by 8 PM. From 9 PM to 2 AM, there's

Good Luck Charms

Arubans take myths and superstitions very seriously. They flinch if a black butterfly flits into their home, since this symbolizes death. They gasp if a child crawls under their legs, since it's a sign that the baby won't grow anymore. And on New Year's Eve, they toss the first sips of whiskey, rum, or champagne from the first bottle that's opened in the new year out the door of their house to show respect to those who have died and to wish luck on others. It's no surprise, then, that good luck charms are part of Aruba's casino culture as well.

The island's most common good luck charm is the djucu (pronounced joo-koo), a brown-and-black stone that comes from the sea and becomes hot when rubbed. They're sold at the convenience store near the Natural Bridge, and many people have them put in gold settings—with their initials engraved in the metal—and wear them around their necks on a chain with other charms such as an anchor or a cross. Another item that's thought to bring good luck is a small bag of sand. Women wear them tucked discreetly in their bras; one woman who visited Aruba every year always carried a few cloves of garlic in her bag. On a recent visit, she removed the garlic, placed it on a slot machine, and won $1,000 instantly. All the more reason to save the scraps from your salad plate when you leave dinner.

live music at the stage near the bar. You'll find it hard to steal away from the pulsating mix of Latin and American tunes. Don't forget to register for free dinners and brunches and hotel discounts at the hostess station. The casino is open until 4 AM. J. E. Irausquin Blvd. 85, Palm Beach, tel. 297/8–61234, www.hyatt.com.

CRYSTAL CASINO. Adorned with Austrian crystal chandeliers and gold-leaf columns, the Aruba Sonesta Resort's casino evokes Monaco's grand establishments—hence, the international clientele. The Salon Privé offers serious gamblers a private room for baccarat, roulette, and high-stakes blackjack. This casino is popular among cruise ship passengers, who stroll over from the port to watch and play in slot tournaments and bet on sporting events. The Crystal Lounge, which overlooks the casino, serves up live music along with the cocktails, and the Crystal Theatre's show, "Let's Go Latin," features an energetic cast of singers and dancers. L. G. Smith Blvd. 82, Oranjestad, tel. 297/8–36000, www. arubasonesta.com.

EXCELSIOR CASINO. The Holiday Inn SunSpree Aruba Beach Resort's casino—the birthplace of Caribbean stud poker—has blackjack, craps, and roulette tables, plenty of slot machines, and a bar featuring live entertainment. There's also a poker room for Texas hold 'em, seven-card stud, and Caribbean stud. It's the only casino on Palm Beach with an ATM adjacent to the cashier. Afternoon bingo overtakes the main floor every day. The casino is open daily from 8 AM to 4 AM. J. E. Irausquin Blvd. 230, Palm Beach, tel. 297/8–67777, www.holidayinn-aruba.com.

RADISSON ARUBA RESORT & CASINO. Although it measures 16,000 square ft, you may have a hard time locating this casino. Descend the stairs at the corner of the resort's lobby, following the sounds of the piano player's tunes. The nightly action here includes Las Vegas–style blackjack, roulette, craps, and slot machines. Overhead, thousands of lights simulate shooting stars that seem destined to carry out your wishes for riches. A host of shops and restaurants let you to chip away at your newfound wealth. The slots here open daily at 10 AM, while the table action begins at 4 PM. Everything shuts down at 4 AM. J. E. Irausquin Blvd. 81, Palm Beach, tel. 297/8–64045, www.radisson.com.

ROYAL CABANA CASINO. The largest casino in the Caribbean, Royal Cabana has a sleek interior that holds more than 400 slot machines. If you like bingo, the casino offers the highest-stakes games around. The Tropicana Showroom features the hit show "Don't Tell Mama," in which female impersonators perform as Cher, Madonna, Whitney Houston, Bette Midler, Whoopi Goldberg, and Joan Rivers. Performances take place Tuesday and Thursday at 9 PM and Wednesday, Friday and Saturday at 10 PM. The slots here open at daily at 11 AM, the tables at 5 or 6 PM. The casino, in the La Cabana All Suite Beach Resort, closes between 3 AM and 4 AM. J. E. Irausquin Blvd. 250, Eagle Beach, tel. 297/8–74665 or 75001, www.lacabana.com.

SEAPORT CASINO. The gambling is low-key at this waterside establishment adjacent to the Aruba Sonesta Suites, the Seaport Marketplace, and the Seaport Conference Center. More than 200 slot machines are in daily operation from 10 AM to 4 AM, and tables are open from 4 PM to 4 AM. From here, you can see the boats on the ocean and enjoy not only the games you'd find at other casinos but also shops, restaurants, bars, and movie theaters. Stop by on Tuesday, Thursday, or Sunday for the casino's popular bingo games. L. G. Smith Blvd. 9, Oranjestad, tel. 297/8–35027 ext. 4212, or 36000.

STELLARIS CASINO. The Aruba Marriott Resort's casino has mirrors on the ceilings that reflect the glamorous chandeliers. Start at the slots at noon or the tables at 4 PM and play until 4 AM if you're on a roll. Take your pick of craps, roulette, Caribbean stud poker, minibaccarat, and superbuck (like blackjack with suits). Every night except Sunday there's a performance by Angelo, billed as Aruba's Ricky Martin, that will keep your spirits up no matter how your luck is going. Check in with the casino when you arrive at the hotel and you'll get a membership card.

If you play high enough stakes at the tables you can win free meals and other prizes. If not, you'll at least get a postcard in the mail offering a special rate on future stays. The hotel offers a 30% discount to those who play at least four hours each day. *L. G. Smith Blvd. 101, Palm Beach, tel. 297/8–69000, www.marriott.com.*

THE GAMES

For a short-form handbook on the rules, the odds, and the strategies for the most popular casino games—or for help deciding on the kind of action that suits your style—read on.

The first part of any casino strategy is to risk the most money on wagers that present the lowest edge for the house. Blackjack, craps, video poker, and baccarat are the most advantageous to the bettor. The two types of bets at baccarat have a house advantage of a little more than 1%. The basic line bets at craps, if backed up with full odds, can be as low as ½%. Blackjack and video poker can not only put you even with the house (a true 50-50 proposition) but give you a slight long-term advantage.

How can a casino provide you with a 50-50 or even a positive expectation at some of its games? First, because a vast number of suckers make bad bets (those with a house advantage of 5%–35%, such as roulette, keno, and slots). Second, because the casino knows that very few people are aware of the opportunities to beat the odds. Third, because it takes skill to exploit these opportunities. However, a mere hour or two spent learning strategies for the beatable games will put you ahead of most visitors who give the gambling industry an average 12%–15% profit margin.

BACCARAT

The most "glamorous" game in the casino, baccarat is a version of *chemin de fer*, which is popular in European gambling halls. It's a favorite with high rollers because thousands of dollars are often staked on one hand. The Italian word *baccara* means "zero." This refers to the point value of 10s and picture cards. The game is run by four pit personnel. Two dealers sit side by side at the middle of the table. They handle the winning and losing bets and keep track of each player's "commission" (explained below). The "caller" stands in the middle of the other side of the table and dictates the action. The ladderman supervises the game and acts as final judge if any disputes arise.

How to Play

Baccarat is played with eight decks of cards dealt from a large "shoe" (or cardholder). Each player is offered a turn at handling the shoe and dealing the cards. Two two-card hands are dealt, the "player" and the "bank" hands. The player who deals the cards is called the banker, although the house banks both hands. The players bet on which hand—player or banker—will come closest to adding up to 9 (a "natural"). Ace through 9 retain face value, while 10s and picture cards are worth zero. If you have a hand adding up to more than 10, the number 10 is subtracted from the total. For example, if one hand contains a 10 and a 4, the hand adds up to 4. If the other holds an ace and a 6, it adds up to 7. If a hand has a 7 and a 9, it adds up to 6.

Depending on the two hands, the caller either declares a winner and loser (if either hand actually adds up to 8 or 9) or calls for another card for the player hand (if it totals 1, 2, 3, 4, 5, or 10). The bank hand then either stands pat or draws a card, determined by a complex series of rules depending on what the player's total is and dictated by the caller. When one or the other hand is declared a winner, the dealers go into action to pay off the winning wagers, collect the losing wagers, and add up the commission (usually 5%) that the house collects on the bank hand. Both bets have a house advantage of slightly more than 1%.

The player-dealer (or banker) holds the shoe as long as the bank hand wins. When the player hand wins, the shoe moves counterclockwise around the table. Players can refuse the shoe and pass it to the next player. Because the caller dictates the action, player responsibilities are minimal. It's not necessary to know the card-drawing rules, even if you're the banker.

Baccarat Strategy

To bet you only have to place your money in the bank, player, or tie box on the layout, which appears directly in front of where you sit. If you're betting that the bank hand will win, you put your chips in the bank box; bets for the player hand go in the player box. (Only real suckers bet on the tie.) Most players bet on the bank hand when they deal, since they "represent" the bank and to do otherwise would seem as if they were betting "against" themselves. This isn't really true, but it seems that way. Playing baccarat is a simple matter of guessing whether the player or banker hand will come closest to 9 and deciding how much to bet on the outcome.

BLACKJACK

How to Play

You play blackjack against a dealer, and whichever of you comes closest to a card total of 21 wins. Number cards are worth their face value, picture cards are worth 10, and aces are worth either 1 or 11. (Hands with aces are known as "soft" hands. Always count the ace first as an 11. If you also have a 10, your total will be 21, not 11.) If the dealer has a 17 and you have a 16, you lose. If you have an 18 against a dealer's 17, you win (even money). If both you and the dealer have a 17, it's a tie (or "push") and no money changes hands. If you go over a total of 21 (or "bust"), you lose, even if the dealer also busts later in the hand. If your first two cards add up to 21 (a "natural"), you're paid 3 to 2.

However, if the dealer also has a natural, it's a push. A natural beats a total of 21 achieved with more than two cards.

You're dealt two cards, either face down or face up, depending on the custom of the casino. The dealer also gives herself two cards, one face down and one face up (except in double-exposure blackjack, where both the dealer's cards are visible). Depending on your first two cards and the dealer's up card, you can **STAND,** or refuse to take another card. You can **HIT,** or take as many cards as you need until you stand or bust. You can **DOUBLE DOWN,** or double your bet and take one card. You can **SPLIT** a like pair; if you're dealt two 8s, for example, you can double your bet and play the 8s as if they're two hands. You can **BUY INSURANCE** if the dealer is showing an ace. Here you're wagering half your initial bet that the dealer *does* have a natural. If so, you lose your initial bet but are paid 2 to 1 on the insurance (which means the whole thing is a push). You can **SURRENDER** half your initial bet if you're holding a bad hand (known as a "stiff") such as a 15 or 16 against a high-up card like a 9 or 10.

Blackjack Strategy

Many people devote a great deal of time to learning complicated statistical schemes. However, if you don't have the time, energy, or inclination to get that seriously involved, the following basic strategies should allow you to play the game with a modicum of skill and a paucity of humiliation:

When your hand is a stiff (a total of 12, 13, 14, 15, or 16) and the dealer shows a 2, 3, 4, 5, or 6, always stand.

When your hand is a stiff and the dealer shows a 7, 8, 9, 10, or ace, always hit.

When you hold 17, 18, 19, or 20, always stand.

When you hold a 10 or 11 and the dealer shows a 2, 3, 4, 5, 6, 7, 8, or 9, always double down.

When you hold a pair of aces or a pair of 8s, always split.

Never buy insurance.

CRAPS

Craps is a dice game played at a large rectangular table with rounded corners. Up to 12 players can stand around the table. The layout is mounted at the bottom of a surrounding "rail," which prevents the dice from being thrown off the table and provides an opposite wall against which to bounce the dice. It can require up to four pit personnel to run an action-packed, fast-paced game of craps. Two dealers handle the bets made on either side of the layout. A "stickman" wields the long wooden "stick," curved at one end, which is used to move the dice around the table. The stickman also calls the number that's rolled and books the proposition bets made in the middle of the layout. The "boxman" sits between the two dealers, overseeing the game and settling any disputes.

How to Play

Stand at the table wherever you can find an open space. You can start betting casino chips immediately, but you have to wait your turn to be the shooter. The dice are passed clockwise around the table (the stickman will give you the dice at the appropriate time). It's important, when you're the "shooter," to roll the dice hard enough so they bounce off the end wall of the table. This shows that you're not trying to control the dice with a "soft roll."

Craps Strategy

Playing craps is fairly straightforward; it's the betting that's complicated. The basic concepts are as follows: If the first time the shooter rolls the dice he or she turns up a 7 or 11, that's called a "natural"—an automatic win. If a 2, 3, or 12 comes up on the first throw (called the "come-out roll"), that's termed "craps"—an automatic lose. Each of the numbers 4, 5, 6, 8, 9, or 10 on a first roll is known as a "point": The shooter keeps rolling the dice until the point comes up again. If a 7 turns up before the point does, that's another loser. When either the point or a losing 7 is rolled, this is known as a "decision," which happens on average every 3.3 rolls.

But "winning" and "losing" rolls of the dice are entirely relative in this game, because there are two ways you can bet at craps: "for" the shooter or "against" the shooter. Betting for means that the shooter will "make his point" (win). Betting against means that the shooter will "seven out" (lose). Either way, you're actually betting against the house, which books all wagers. If you're betting "for" on the come-out, you place your chips on the layout's "pass line." If a 7 or 11 is rolled, you win even money. If a 2, 3, or 12 (craps) is rolled, you lose your bet. If you're betting "against" on the come-out, you place your chips in the "don't pass bar." A 7 or 11 loses; a 2, 3, or 12 wins. A shooter can bet for or against himself, herself, or against other players.

There are also roughly two dozen wagers you can make on any single specific roll of the dice. Craps strategy books can give you the details on come/don't come, odds, place, buy, big six, field, and proposition bets.

ROULETTE

Roulette is a casino game that utilizes a perfectly balanced wheel with 38 numbers (0, 00, and 1 through 36), a small white ball, a large layout with 11 different betting options, and special "wheel chips." The layout organizes 11 different bets into six "inside bets" (the single numbers, or those closest to the dealer) and five "outside bets" (the grouped bets, or those closest to the players).

The dealer spins the wheel clockwise and the ball counterclockwise. When the ball slows, the dealer announces,

"No more bets." The ball drops from the "back track" to the "bottom track," caroming off built-in brass barriers and bouncing in and out of the different cups in the wheel before settling into the cup of the winning number. Then the dealer places a marker on the number and scoops all the losing chips into her corner. Depending on how crowded the game is, the casino can count on roughly 50 spins of the wheel per hour.

How to Play

To buy in, place your cash on the layout near the wheel. Inform the dealer of the denomination of the individual unit you intend to play. Know the table limits (displayed on a sign in the dealer area). Don't ask for a 25¢ denomination if the minimum is $1. The dealer gives you a stack of wheel chips of a different color from those of all the other players and places a chip marker atop one of your wheel chips on the rim of the wheel to identify its denomination. Note that you must cash in your wheel chips at the roulette table before you leave the game. Only the dealer can verify how much they're worth.

Roulette Strategy

INSIDE BETS

With inside bets, you can lay any number of chips (depending on the table limits) on a single number, 1 through 36 or o or oo. If the number hits, your payoff is 35 to 1, for a return of $36. You could, conceivably, place a $1 chip on all 38 numbers, but the return of $36 would leave you $2 short, which divides out to 5.26%, the house advantage. If you place a chip on the line between two numbers and one of those numbers hits, you're paid 17 to 1 for a return of $18 (again, $2 short of the true odds). Betting on three numbers returns 11 to 1, four numbers returns 8 to 1, five numbers pays 6 to 1 (this is the worst bet at roulette, with a 7.89% disadvantage), and six numbers pays 5 to 1.

OUTSIDE BETS

To place an outside bet, lay a chip on one of three "columns" at the lower end of the layout next to numbers 34, 35, and 36. This pays 2 to 1. A bet placed in the first 12, second 12, or third 12 boxes also pays 2 to 1. A bet on red or black, odd or even, and 1 through 18 or 19 through 36 pays off at even money, 1 to 1. If you think you can bet on red *and* black, or odd *and* even, in order to play roulette and drink for free all night, think again. The green 0 or 00, which fail outside these two basic categories, will come up on average once every 19 spins of the wheel.

SLOT MACHINES

Around the turn of 20th century, Charlie Fey built the first slot in his San Francisco basement. Today hundreds of models accept everything from pennies to specially minted $500 tokens. The major advance in the game is the progressive jackpot. Banks of slots within a casino are connected by computer, and the jackpot total is displayed on a digital meter above the machines. Generally, the total increases by 5% of the wager. If you're playing a dollar machine, each time you pull the handle (or press the spin button), a nickel is added to the jackpot.

How to Play

To play, insert your penny, nickel, quarter, silver dollar, or dollar token into the slot at the far right edge of the machine. Pull the handle or press the spin button, and then wait for the reels to spin and stop one by one and for the machine to determine whether you're a winner (occasionally) or a loser (the rest of the time). It's pretty simple, but because there are so many types of machines nowadays, be sure you know exactly how the one you're playing operates.

Slot-Machine Strategy

The house advantage on slots varies from machine to machine, between 3% and 25%. Casinos that advertise a 97% payback are telling you that at least one of their slot machines has a house advantage of 3%. Which one? There's really no way of knowing. Generally, $1 machines pay back at a higher percentage than quarter or nickel machines. On the other hand, machines with smaller jackpots pay back more money more frequently, meaning that you'll be playing with more of your winnings.

One of the all-time great myths about slot machines is that they're "due" for a jackpot. Slots, like roulette, craps, keno, and Big Six, are subject to the Law of Independent Trials, which means the odds are permanently and unalterably fixed. If the odds of lining up three sevens on a 25¢ slot machine have been set by the casino at 1 in 10,000, then those odds remain 1 in 10,000 whether the three 7s have been hit three times in a row or not hit for 90,000 plays. Don't waste a lot of time playing a machine that you suspect is "ready," and don't think if someone hits a jackpot on a particular machine only minutes after you've finished playing on it that it was "yours."

VIDEO POKER

Like blackjack, video poker is a game of strategy and skill, and at select times on select machines, the player actually holds the advantage, however slight, over the house. Unlike with slot machines, you can determine the exact edge of video poker machines. Like slots, however, video poker machines are often tied into a progressive meter; when the jackpot total reaches high enough, you can beat the casino at its own game. The variety of video poker machines is growing steadily. All are played in similar fashion, but the strategies are different. This section deals only with straight-draw video poker.

How to Play

The schedule for the payback on winning hands is posted on the machine, usually above the screen. It lists the returns for a high pair (generally jacks or better), two pair, three of a kind, a flush, full house, straight flush, four of a kind, and royal flush, depending on the number of coins played—usually 1, 2, 3, 4, or 5. Look for machines that pay with a single coin played: 1 coin for "jacks or better" (meaning a pair of jacks, queens, kings, or aces; any other pair is a stiff), 2 coins for two pairs, 3 for three of a kind, 6 for a flush, 9 for a full house, 50 for a straight flush, 100 for four of a kind, and 250 for a royal flush. This is known as a 9/6 machine—one that gives a nine-coin payback for the full house and a six-coin payback for the flush with one coin played. Other machines are known as 8/5 (8 for the full house, 5 for the flush), 7/5, and 6/5.

You want a 9/6 machine because it gives you the best odds: the return from a standard 9/6 straight-draw machine is 99.5%; you give up only half a percent to the house. An 8/5 machine returns 97.3%. On 6/5 machines, the figure drops to 95.1%, slightly less than roulette. Machines with varying paybacks are scattered throughout the casinos. In some you'll see an 8/5 machine right next to a 9/6, and someone will be blithely playing the 8/5 machine!

As with slot machines, it's optimum to play the maximum number of coins to qualify for the jackpot. You insert five coins into the slot and press the "deal" button. Five cards appear on the screen—say, 5, jack, queen, 5, 9. To hold the pair of 5s, you press the hold buttons under the first and fourth cards. The word "hold" appears underneath the two 5s. You then press the "draw" button (often the same button as "deal") and three new cards appear on the screen—say, 10, jack, 5. You have three 5s. With five coins bet, the machine will give you 15 credits. Now you can press the "max bet" button: five units will be removed from your credits, and five new cards will appear on the screen. You repeat the hold and draw process; if you hit a winning hand, the proper payback will be added to your credits. Those who want coins rather than credit can hit the "cash out" button at any time. Some machines don't have credit counters and automatically dispense coins for a winning hand.

Video-Poker Strategy

Like blackjack, video poker has a basic strategy that's been formulated by the computer simulation of hundreds of millions of hands. The most effective way to learn it is with a video poker computer program that deals the cards on your screen, then tutors you in how to play each hand properly. If you don't want to devote that much time to the study of video poker, memorizing these six rules will help you make the right decision for more than half the hands you'll be dealt:

If you're dealt a completely "stiff" hand (no like cards and no picture cards), draw five new cards.

If you're dealt a hand with no like cards but with one jack, queen, king, or ace, always hold on to the picture card; if you're dealt two different picture cards, hold both. But if you're dealt three different picture cards, hold only two (the two of the same suit, if that's an option).

If you're dealt a pair, hold it, no matter the face value.

Never hold a picture card with a pair of 2s through 10s.

Never draw two cards to try for a straight or a flush.

Never draw one card to try for an inside straight.

Clouds fill the sky and a cool breeze blows as the boat arrives to pick up a group of snorkelers. They board reluctantly, and their hopes of having an underwater adventure dim as the skies open in a dramatic downpour. The boat's bartenders mix up some "captain's specials" and turn the island music up a notch. This elicits smiles all around, and the skies seem to brighten. In no time, the sun is shining again, launching another beautiful day in the great outdoors.

In This Chapter

outdoor activities and sports

ABOVE THE SURFACE AND BELOW, Aruban waters are brimming with activity. Although beach bumming is a popular pastime, tennis, horseback riding, golf, and fishing are also good options. More adventurous souls can explore on a motorcycle, parasail with the ocean breezes, or leap through the air on a skydive. Constant trade winds have made Aruba an internationally recognized windsurfing destination. The crystalline waters of the island's leeward side offer scuba divers and snorkelers a kaleidoscopic adventure day or night.

You probably won't find Arubans singing "Take Me Out to the Ball Game," but come time for soccer season (late May–November, with matches on Tuesday, Thursday, Saturday, and Sunday) or track-and-field meets and some 3,200 spirited people pack into the **COMPLEHO DEPORTIVO G. P. TRINIDAD** (Stadionweg, Oranjestad, tel. 297/8–27488). Events at this complex open with the Aruban national anthem, a display of flags, and the introduction of any old-timers in the stadium. Admission ranges from $3 to $6, depending on whether it's a local or international competition. Regardless of what's on, you won't find vendors hawking hot dogs or cotton candy. The snack bar sells such Aruban favorites as *pastechi* (meat, cheese, or seafood-filled turnovers) or *bitterballen* (meatballs) that you can wash down with a soda or a local Balashi beer.

Sidney Ponson: Pitcher

"My life was the beach before baseball," says Sidney Ponson, who started playing ball in Aruba at 9 and signed with the minor leagues at 16 before becoming a right-handed pitcher for the Baltimore Orioles in 1998. Now, he spends 10 months a year in the United States playing and training (his grueling workouts last from 7:30 AM to 1 PM and involve lifting weights, running, and throwing), and two months in Aruba resting and visiting family and friends.

The island celebrity, who idolized Roger Clemens throughout his childhood, says he had fun growing up in Aruba, where he loved to sail, scuba dive, and play soccer and volleyball. Baseball was his first passion, though it wasn't easy to play on this dry island, with fields full of rocks. But employment on his uncle's boat taught him to work hard for what he wanted in life.

Hitting the big leagues involved lots of hard work, but it was worth it when he got the call to play. "It was 6:30 AM, and I was on a road trip in a hotel in Scranton," he remembers. "They told me when to show up and said to be ready to play at 8:30." Now there are three other Aruban ballplayers playing in the U.S. (Calvin Maduro, who also plays for the Baltimore Orioles, and Eugene Kingshill and Radames Dijkhoff, who play for Triple A teams), and it won't be long before there are more.

To prepare for a game, Ponson heads to the clubhouse for some serious stretching to the hard rock music of Metallica, AC/DC, or Mötley Crüe. How does it feel right before he heads out to pitch? "One million people want to do what I do," says Pinson, "play ball in front of 50,000 people every night, and that's a great feeling."

BEACHES

The beaches on Aruba are legendary: white sand, turquoise waters, and virtually no litter—everyone takes the NO TIRA SUSHI (NO LITTERING) signs very seriously, especially considering the island's $280 fine. The major beaches, which back up to the hotels along the southwestern strip, are public and crowded. Make sure you're well protected from the sun—it scorches fast despite the cooling trade winds. Luckily, there's at least one covered bar (and often an ice cream stand) at virtually every hotel. On the island's northeastern side, wind makes the waters too choppy for swimming, but the vistas are great and the terrain is wonderful for exploring.

ARASHI BEACH. The water is calm, the swimming is fine, and the white, powdery sands are shaded by some huts (though there are no other facilities). The beach is a 10-minute walk from the last bus stop on Malmok Beach and is accessible by car or taxi.

BABY BEACH. On the island's eastern tip, this semicircular beach borders a bay that's as placid and just about as shallow as a wading pool—perfect for tots, shore divers, and terrible swimmers. Thatched shaded areas are good for cooling off. Stop by the nearby snack truck for burgers, hot dogs, beer, and soda.

BOCA CATALINA. Although there are some stones and pebbles along this white-sand beach, snorkelers come for the shallow water filled with fish. Swimmers will also appreciate the calm conditions. There aren't any facilities nearby, however, so pack provisions.

BOCA GRANDI. Strong swimming skills are a must at this beach near the island's eastern tip.

BOCA PRINS. You'll need a four-wheel-drive vehicle to make the trek here. The beach is about as large as a Brazilian bikini, but with two rocky cliffs and crashing waves, it's as romantic as you can imagine. Boca Prins is also famous for its backdrop of enormous vanilla-sand dunes. This isn't a swimming beach, however. Bring a picnic, a beach blanket, and sturdy sneakers, and descend the rocks that form steps to the water's edge.

BOCA TABLA. This east-side beach, also known as Bachelor's Beach, is known for the white-powder sand and the good snorkeling and windsurfing. Don't head here for the swimming (conditions aren't the best) or the facilities (there aren't any).

DOS PLAYA. Hire a four-wheel-drive vehicle, pack a blanket and a picnic basket, and head here to take in the beautiful view. Swimming is discouraged because of strong currents and massive waves.

DRUIF. Fine white sand and calm water makes this "tops-optional" beach a fine choice for sunbathing and swimming. Convenience is a highlight, too: hotels are close at hand, and the beach is accessible by public bus as well as rental car or taxi.

EAGLE BEACH. On the southwestern coast, across the highway from what is quickly becoming known as Time-Share Lane, is what was designated one of the top 10 beaches around the globe in 2001, according to the authors of *Dream Beaches of the World*. Not long ago it was a nearly deserted stretch of pristine sand dotted with the occasional thatched picnic hut. Now that the resorts are completed, this mile-plus-long beach hops.

FISHERMAN'S HUT. This beach, also called Hadikurari, is a windsurfer's haven. In fact, it's the site for the annual Hi-Winds Pro-Am Windsurfing Competition. But any day you can take a picnic lunch (tables are available) and watch the elegant purple, aqua, and orange sails struggle in the wind. The swimming conditions are good here as well, though the sand has some pebbles and stones.

GRAPEFIELD BEACH. To the northeast of San Nicolas, this sweep of blinding white sand in the shadow of cliffs and boulders is marked by a statue of an anchor dedicated to all seamen. Pick sea grapes in high season (January–June). Swim at your own risk; the waves here can be rough.

MALMOK BEACH. On the northwestern shore, this small, nondescript beach (where some of Aruba's wealthiest families have built tony residences) borders shallow waters that stretch 300 yards from shore. It's the perfect place to learn to windsurf. Right off the coast here is a favorite haunt for divers and snorkelers—the wreck of the German ship *Antilla*, scuttled in 1940.

MANCHEBO BEACH. In front of the Manchebo Beach Resort, this impressively wide stretch of white powder, also called Punta Brabo, is where officials turn a blind eye to the occasional topless sunbathers.

MANGEL HALTO. Drive or cab it over to this east-side beach, also known as Savaneta. It's a lovely setting for a picnic. Hop into the shallow waters for a swim after taking in the sun on the fine white sand.

PALM BEACH. This stretch runs from the Wyndham Aruba Beach Resort and Casino to the Marriott Aruba Ocean Club. It's the center of Aruban tourism, offering the best in swimming, sailing, and other water sports. In some spots you might find a variety of shells that are great to collect, but not as much fun to step on barefoot—bring sandals just in case.

RODGER'S BEACH. Next to Baby Beach on the island's eastern tip, this is a beautiful curving stretch of sand only slightly marred by the view of the oil refinery at the bay's far side. Swimming conditions are excellent here, and the snack bar offers live entertainment at the water's edge.

SANTO LARGO. Swimming conditions are good—thanks to shallow water edged by white powder sand—but there are no facilities here.

SURFSIDE. Accessible by public bus, car, or taxi, this beach is the perfect place to swim. It's also conveniently located next to the Havana Beach Club and across the street from the Caribbean Town Beach Resort.

ACTIVITIES

Adventure Games

Paint-ball aficionados can unite in spirited versions of capture the flag. The game is played with an air gun that propels a biodegradable gelatin capsule that splatters you with water-soluble paint on impact. To win, simply return the opposing team's flag to your own team's station without being hit by a pellet. Games (complete with equipment and protective gear) are run by **EVENTS IN MOTION** (Rancho Daimari, Tanki Leendert 249, Plantage Daimari, tel. 297/8–75675, www.visitaruba.com/ranchodaimari). They begin every morning and last about two hours, costing $35 per person with a minimum of 10 people. You must make reservations three days in advance.

Biking and Motorcycling

Pedal pushing is a great way to get around the island; the climate is perfect, and the trade winds help to keep you cool. **PABLITO'S BIKE RENTAL** (L. G. Smith Blvd. 234, Oranjestad, tel. 297/8–78655) rents mountain bikes for $15 per day.

If you prefer to exert less energy while reaping the rewards of the outdoors, a scooter is a great way to whiz from place to place. Or let your hair down completely and cruise around on a Harley Davidson. **BIG TWIN ARUBA** (L. G. Smith Blvd. 124-A, Oranjestad, tel. 297/8–28660, www.harleydavidson-aruba.com), open Monday through Saturday from 9 to 6, rents motorcycles to fulfill every biker's fantasy. With an initial $500 deposit, rates are $100–$150 for a day, or $55–$95 for a half day. The dealership also sells Harley clothing, accessories, and collectibles. Be sure to pose for a photo next to the classic 1939 Liberator on display in the showroom.

There are plenty of dealers around who will be happy to help you in your motoring pursuits. For Yamaha scooters and ATVs, contact **GEORGE'S CYCLE CENTER** (L. G. Smith Blvd. 124, Oranjestad, tel. 297/9–32202). **DONATA CAR AND CYCLE** (Catiri 59, Tanki Leendert, tel. 297/8–34343) rents motorcycles, mopeds, and scooters. **SEMVER CYCLE RENTAL** (Noord 22, Noord, tel. 297/8–66851 or 66853) will help you choose the motorcycle or scooter that matches your experience level and your plans for the day.

Bowling

The **EAGLE BOWLING PALACE** (Sasakiweg, Pos Abou, Oranjestad, tel. 297/8–35038) has 16 lanes, a cocktail lounge, and a snack bar; it's open daily 10 AM to 2 AM. One lane for one hour will cost $8.50–$11.50, depending on the time of day.

Fishing

Deep-sea catches here include barracuda, kingfish, blue and white marlin, wahoo, bonito, and black and yellow tuna. Each October, the island hosts the International White Marlin Competition. Many skippered charter boats are available for half- or full-day sails. Packages include tackle, bait, and refreshments. Prices range from $220 to $320 for a half-day charter and from $400 to $600 for a full day. Contact **DE PALM TOURS** (L. G. Smith Blvd. 142, Oranjestad, tel. 297/8–24400 or 800/766–6016, www.depalm.com) for a number of fishing options. **PELICAN TOURS & WATERSPORTS** (J. E. Irausquin Blvd. 232, Palm Beach, tel. 297/8–72302, www.pelican-aruba.com) is not just for the surf and snorkel crowd; the company will help you catch one that didn't get away. **RED SAIL SPORTS** (J. E. Irausquin Blvd. 83,

Oranjestad, tel. 297/8–61603 or 877/733–7245 in the U.S., www.aruba-redsail.com) will arrange everything for your fishing trip. **TEASER CHARTERS** (St. Vincentweg 5, Oranjestad, tel. 297/ 8–25088, www.teasercharters.com) offers the hook and line, but the sinker is up to you.

Golf

Golf may seem incongruous on an arid island like Aruba, yet there are two courses. The constant trade winds and occasional stray goat add unexpected hazards.

ARUBA GOLF CLUB (Golfweg 82, near San Nicolas, tel. 297/8–42006) has a 9-hole course with 20 sand traps and five water traps, roaming goats, and lots of cacti. There are 11 greens covered with artificial turf, making 18-hole tournaments a possibility. The clubhouse has a bar and locker rooms. Greens fees are $10 for nine holes, $15 for 18 holes. Golf carts are available.

TIERRA DEL SOL (Malmokweg, tel. 297/8–60978) is on the northwest coast near the California Lighthouse. Designed by Robert Trent Jones Jr., this 18-hole championship course combines Aruba's native beauty—cacti and rock formations—with the lush greens of the world's best courses. The three knockouts are Hole 3, perched on a cliff overlooking the sea; Hole 14, with a saltwater marsh inhabited by wild egrets; and Hole 16, whose fairway rolls along dunes. The $130 greens fee includes a golf cart equipped with a communications system that allows you to order drinks that will be ready upon your return. Half-day golf clinics, a bargain at $45, include lunch in the clubhouse. The pro shop is one of the Caribbean's most elegant, with an extremely attentive staff. Package vacations with villa rentals are available.

Two elevated 18-hole miniature golf courses surrounded by a moat are available at **JOE MENDEZ MINIATURE ADVENTURE**

GOLF (Sasakiweg, Noord, tel. 297/8–76625). There are also paddleboats and bumper boats, a bar, and a snack stand. A round of 18 holes costs $6.50. It's open 5 PM to 1 AM during the week and from noon to 1 AM on the weekends.

ARUBA GOLF & LEISURE (J. E. Irasquin Blvd. 326, Oranjestad, tel. 297/8–64589) is the site of a 300-yard driving range, an 18-hole putting green, and a chipping area. Pay $3.50 for a 35 bucket of balls and $10 for a half-set of rental clubs. It's open from 7:30 AM to 11 PM daily.

Hiking

There are more than 34 km (20 mi) of trails in **ARIKOK NATIONAL PARK,** concentrated in island's eastern interior and along its northeast coast. The park is crowned by Aruba's second highest mountain, the 577-ft Mt. Arikok, so climbing is also a possibility.

Hiking in the park, whether alone or in a group led by guides, is generally not too strenuous. Look for different colors to determine the degree of difficulty of each trail. Sturdy shoes are a must to grip the granular surfaces and climb the occasionally steep terrain. You should also exercise caution with the strong sun—bring along plenty of water and wear sunscreen and a hat.

The Aruban government is working on a 10-year ecotourism plan to preserve the resources of the park, which makes up 18% of the island's total area. The effort includes setting aside areas for recreation, establishing zones where the natural habitats are protected, and developing a scenic loop roadway. At the park's main entrance, the Arikok Center will house offices, rest rooms, and food facilities. Under the new plan, all visitors will have to stop here upon entering so that officials can manage the traffic flow and distribute information on park rules and features.

DE PALM TOURS (L. G. Smith Blvd. 142, Oranjestad, tel. 297/8–24400 or 800/766–6016, www.depalm.com) offers a guided

Wildlife Watching

Wildlife abounds on Aruba. Look for the cottontail rabbit: the black patch on its neck likens it to a species found in Venezuela, spawning a theory that it was brought to the island by pre-Columbian peoples. Wild donkeys, originally transported to the island by the Spanish, are found in the more rugged terrain; sheep and goats roam freely throughout the island.

About 170 bird species make their home on Aruba year-round, and migratory birds temporarily raise the total to 300 species when they fly by in November and January. Among the highlights are: the trupiaal (which is bright orange), the prikichi (a parakeet with a green body and yellow head), and the barika geel (a small, yellow-bellied bird with a sweet tooth—you may find one eating the sugar off your breakfast table). At Bubali Bird Sanctuary on the island's western side, you can see various types of waterfowl, especially cormorants, herons, scarlet ibis, and fish eagles. Along the south shore, brown pelicans are common. At Tierra del Sol golf course in the north, you may glimpse the shoko, the endangered burrowing owl.

Lizard varieties include large iguanas, once hunted for use in local soups and stews. (That practice is now illegal.) Like chameleons, these iguanas change color to adapt to their surroundings—from bright green when foraging in the foliage (which they love to eat) to a brownish shade when sunning themselves in the dirt. The pega pega—a cousin of the gecko—is named for the suction pads on its feet that allow it to grip virtually any surface (pega means "to stick" in Papiamento). The kododo blauw (whiptail lizard) is one of the species that is unique to the island.

There are two types of snakes found only on Aruba. The cat-eyed santanero isn't venomous, but it won't hesitate to defecate in your hand should you pick it up. The poisonous cascabel is a unique subspecies of rattlesnake that doesn't use its rattle. These snakes live in the area between Mt. Yamanota, Fontein, and San Nicolas.

three-hour trip to sites of unusual natural beauty that are accessible only on foot. The fee is $25 per person, including refreshments and transportation. A minimum of four people is required.

Horseback Riding

Four ranches offer short jaunts along the beach or longer rides along trails passing through countryside flanked by cacti, divi-divi trees, and aloe vera plants. Ask if you can stop off at Cura di Tortuga, a natural pool that's reputed to have restorative powers. Rides are also possible in the Arikok National Park. Rates run from $25 for an hour-long trip to $65 for a 3½-hour tour. Private rides cost slightly more.

DE PALM TOURS (L. G. Smith Blvd. 142, Oranjestad, tel. 297/8–24400 or 800/766–6016, www.depalm.com) can arrange treks. **RANCHO EL PASO** (Washington 44, tel. 297/8–73310 or 297/8–67165, ranchoelpaso.bizland.com) has seasoned guides that show you Malmok's beautiful beach and the surrounding countryside. Tours, costing $45 per person, head out out daily at 9 AM. **RANCHO DEL CAMPO** (Sombre 22E, Santa Cruz, tel. 297/8–50290, www.ranchodelcampo.com), the first to offer rides to the Natural Pool almost eleven years ago, offers that excursion for $50 per person. **RANCHO DAIMARI** (Plantage Daimari, tel. 297/8–60239, www.visitaruba.com/ranchodaimari) will lead your horse to water—either at Natural Bridge or Natural Pool—in the morning or afternoon for $55 per person. **RANCHO NOTORIOUS** (Boroncana, Noord, tel. 297/8–60508, www.ranchonotorious.com) will take you to the beach to snorkel for $55, on a tour of the countryside for $50, or on a three-hour ride up to the California Lighthouse for $65.

Jet Skiing

For sheer excitement, there's nothing like sputtering around Aruba's aqua-blue water on jet skis. Rentals are available in the water sports centers at most hotels. Average prices for a half-hour ride are $45 for a single jet ski and $55 for a double. There are a few operators on the island, all well-regarded. **DE PALM TOURS** (L. G. Smith Blvd. 142, Oranjestad, tel. 297/8–24400 or 800/766–6016, www.depalm.com) is a well-known water sports operator that offers jet-skiing. **PELICAN TOURS & WATERSPORTS** (J. E. Irausquin Blvd. 232, Palm Beach, tel. 297/8–72302, www.pelican-aruba.com) offers jet-skis and wave runners. The company operates from most major hotels. **RED SAIL SPORTS** (J. E. Irausquin Blvd. 83, Oranjestad, tel. 297/8–61603; 877/733–7245 in the U.S., www.aruba-redsail.com) provides double-seater jet skis through many of the island's hotels. **UNIQUE SPORTS OF ARUBA** (L. G. Smith Blvd. 79, Oranjestad, tel./fax 297/8–60096 or 297/8–63900, www.visitaruba.com/uniquesports) operating exclusively from the Aruba Grand Beach Resort on Palm Beach, rents single and double jet skis.

Kayaking

Kayaking is a popular sport on Aruba, especially because the waters are so calm. It's a great way to explore the coast. Every day except Sunday, **DE PALM TOURS** (L. G. Smith Blvd. 142, Oranjestad, tel. 297/8–24400 or 800/766–6016, www.depalm.com) offers a four-hour guided kayaking tour that also includes some snorkeling. The cost, including lunch, is $65.

Parasailing

For about 12 exhilarating minutes, motorboats from Palm and Eagle beaches tow you up and over the waters around Aruba ($45 for a single-seater, $75 for a tandem). You can make arrangements with your hotel, or through independent operators stationed on the beaches. **CARIBBEAN PARASAIL** (tel. 297/8–60505) is one of the island's top operators. Working with many hotels, **PELICAN TOURS & WATERSPORTS** (tel. 297/8–72302, www.pelican-aruba.com) offers parasailing. Although it's best known for its diving trips, **RED SAIL SPORTS** (tel. 297/8–61603; 877/733–7245 in the U.S., www.aruba-redsail.com) will also take you parasailing.

Sailing

You can have a hull of a good time sailing around Aruba on a Sunfish, or you can opt for a daytime or sunset sail aboard a trimaran or catamaran. The **SEAPORT MARINA** (Seaport Marketplace 204, Oranjestad, tel. 297/8–39190, www.seaportmarinaaruba.com) is the place to go for charters.

DE PALM TOURS (L. G. Smith Blvd. 142, Oranjestad, tel. 297/8–24400 or 800/766–6016, www.depalm.com) will sail you over the open seas for a four-hour snorkeling adventure at nearby reefs. The cost is $54 per person. *MI DUSHI* (Turibana Plaza, Noord 124, Noord, tel. 297/8–62010, www.kukookunuku.com), a ship whose name means "My Sweetheart," will sail you into the sunset with yours for $35 per person. Daytime sails on this romantic two-masted ship include breakfast, lunch, and snorkeling equipment for $69 per person. **PELICAN TOURS & WATERSPORTS** (J. E. Irausquin Blvd. 232, Palm Beach, tel. 297/8–72302, www.pelican-aruba.com), offers day sails with snorkeling to two different reefs for $30 per person. The company also offers sunset sails for the same price that can be combined with dinner at the Pelican Restaurant on Palm Beach. **RED SAIL SPORTS** (J. E. Irausquin Blvd. 83, Oranjestad, tel. 297/8–61603; 877/733–7245 in the U.S., www.aruba-redsail.com) will take you on a day sail, serve you lunch, and let you snorkel at two different sites for $50 per person. A later afternoon trip includes snacks but only one snorkel stop. There's also a sunset cruise for $33 per person.

Scuba Diving and Snorkeling

With visibility of up to 90 ft, the waters around Aruba are excellent for snorkeling and diving. Both advanced and novice divers will find plenty to occupy their time, as many of the most popular sites, including some interesting shipwrecks, are found in shallow waters ranging from 30 ft to 60 ft. Coral reefs covered with sensuously waving sea fans and eerie giant sponge tubes attract a colorful menagerie of sea life, including gliding manta rays, curious sea turtles, shy octopuses, and fish from grunts to groupers. Note that marine preservation is a priority on Aruba, and regulations by the Conference on International Trade in Endangered Species make it unlawful to remove coral, conch, and other marine life from the water.

Most resorts offer diving courses for beginners that include instruction and all equipment; those seeking advanced certification can do so through any of the island's licensed dive centers. Some top dive sites are listed below, but be sure to pick up the Aruba Tourism Authority's brochure, "The Island for Water Sports," which describes many more.

OPERATORS

Expect snorkel gear to rent for about $15 per day and trips to cost around $40. Scuba rates are around $50 for a one-tank reef or wreck dive, $65 for a two-tank dive, and $45 for a night dive. Resort courses, which offer an introduction to scuba diving, average $65 to $70. If you want to go all the way, complete open-water certification costs around $300.

The more seasoned diving crowd might check with **ARUBA PRO DIVE** (Ponton 88, Noord, tel. 297/8–25520, www.arubaprodive. com), for special deals. **DAX DIVERS** (Kibaima 7, Santa Cruz, tel. 297/8–51270) is the operator that boasts an instructor training course. Some dives are less expensive, at $35 for 40 minutes with one tank. **DE PALM TOURS** (L. G. Smith Blvd. 142, Oranjestad, tel. 297/8–24400 or 800/766–6016) is one of the

Find America *with a Compass*

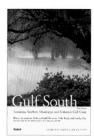

Written by local authors and illustrated throughout with spectacular color images, the Compass American Guides reveal the character and culture of more than 40 of America's most fascinating destinations. Perfect for residents who want to explore their own backyard, and visitors who want an insider's perspective on the history, heritage, and all there is to see and do.

Fodor's COMPASS AMERICAN GUIDES

At bookstores everywhere.

When you pack your MCI Calling Card, it's like packing your loved ones along too.

Your MCI Calling Card is the easy way to stay in touch when you travel. Use it to call to and from over 125 countries. Plus, every time you call, you can earn frequent flier miles. So wherever your travels take you, call home with your MCI Calling Card. It's even easy to get one. Just visit www.mci.com/worldphone or www.mci.com/partners.

EASY TO CALL WORLDWIDE

1 Just enter the WorldPhone® access number of the country you're calling from.

2 Enter or give the operator your MCI Calling Card number.

3 Enter or give the number you're calling.

Argentina	0-800-222-6249
Bermuda ÷	1-800-888-8000
Brazil	0800-890-0012
United States	1-800-888-8000

÷ Limited availability.

EARN FREQUENT FLIER MILES

best options for your undersea experience. Don a helmet and walk along the ocean floor near De Palm Island, home of huge blue parrot fish. Have your picture taken at an underwater table loaded with champagne glasses and roses. Try Snuba—like scuba diving but without the heavy air tanks—either from a boat or from an island. Rates are $79 to $99, including meals. **DIVE ARUBA** (Williamstraat 8, Oranjestad, tel. 297/8–25216, www.divearuba.com) offers resort courses, certification courses, and trips to interesting shipwrecks. **MERMAID SPORT DIVERS** (Manchebo Beach Resort, J. E. Irausquin Blvd. 55A, Eagle Beach, tel. 297/8–35546, www.scubadivers-aruba.com) offers full dive packages with PADI-certified instructors.

NATIVE DIVERS ARUBA (Koyari 1, Noord, tel. 297/8–64763, www.nativedivers.com) offers all types of dives. Courses in specialties such as underwater naturalist are taught by PADI-certified instructors. At **PELICAN TOURS & WATERSPORTS** (J. E. Irausquin Blvd. 232, Palm Beach, tel. 297/8–72302, www.pelican-aruba.com) there are options for divers of all levels. Novices start with mid-morning classes and then move to the pool to practice what they've learned; by afternoon they put their new skills to use at a shipwreck off the coast. **RED SAIL SPORTS** (J. E. Irausquin Blvd. 83, Oranjestad, tel. 297/8–61603 or 877/733–7245 in the U.S., www.aruba-redsail.com) has courses for children and others new to scuba diving. An introductory class costs about $80.

SEARUBA FLY 'N DIVE (Shiribana 9A, Paradera, tel. 297/8–78759, www.visitaruba.com/searuba) will take you higher and lower than you ever thought possible in one day. You can take aerial shots from above the dive sites, then head underwater. Aside from the usual diving courses, the company will instruct your group in rescue techniques for around $350 per person. **UNIQUE SPORTS OF ARUBA** (L. G. Smith Blvd. 79, Oranjestad, tel. 297/8–60096 or 297/8–63900, www.visitaruba.com/uniquesports) lives up to its name, providing dive master, rescue, and certification courses.

DIVE SITES ON THE WEST SIDE

ANTILLA **WRECK.** This German freighter, which sunk off the northwest coast near Malmok Beach, is very popular with both divers and snorkelers. Scuttled during World War II not long after its maiden voyage, the 400-ft-long vessel—referred to by locals as "the ghost ship"—has large compartments. You can climb into the captain's bathtub, which sits beside the wreck, for a unique photo op. Lobster, angelfish, yellow tail, and other fish swim about the wreck, which is blanketed by giant tube sponges and coral.

BARCADERA REEF. Only large types of coral—staghorn, elkhorn, pillar—find their niche close to this reef because the sand makes it difficult for the smaller varieties to survive. The huge (and abundant) sea fans here wave in the current.

BLACK BEACH. The clear waters just off this beach are dotted with sea fans. The area takes its name from the rounded black stones lining the shore. It's the only bay on the island's north coast sheltered from thunderous waves, making it a safe spot for diving.

CALIFORNIAN **WRECK.** The steamer that received—but failed to respond to—SOS signals from the sinking *Titanic* was later stranded on Aruba's rocky northwest coast. Although the ship is submerged at a depth that's perfect for underwater photography, this site is safe only for advanced divers; the currents here are strong, and the waters are dangerously choppy.

HARBOUR REEF. Steeply sloped boulders surrounded by a multitude of soft coral formations make this a great spot for novices. The calm waters are noteworthy for their abundance of fascinating plant life.

MALMOK REEF. Lobsters and stingrays are among the highlights at this bottom reef adorned by giant green, orange, and purple barrel sponges as well as leaf and brain coral. From here you can spot the *Debbie II*, a 120-ft barge that sank in 1992.

PEDERNALES WRECK. During World War II, this oil tanker was torpedoed by a German submarine. The U.S. military cut out the damaged centerpiece, towed the two remaining pieces to the States, and welded them together into a smaller vessel that eventually transported troops during the invasion of Normandy. The section that was left behind in shallow water is now surrounded by coral formations, making this a good site for novice divers. The ship's cabins, wash basins, and pipelines are exposed. The area teems with grouper and angelfish.

SKELETON CAVE. Human bones found here (historians hypothesize that they're remains of ancient Arawak people) gave this dive spot its name. A large piece of broken rock forms the entrance where the cave meets the coast.

SONESTA REEF. Two downed planes are the centerpiece of this interesting dive site near Sonesta Island. Several types of brain coral abound in this sandy-bottomed area.

TUGBOAT WRECK. Spotted eagle rays and stingrays are sometimes observed at this shipwreck at the foot of Harbour Reef, making it one of Aruba's most popular. Spectacular formations of brain, sheet, and star coral blanket the path to the wreck, which is inhabited by a pair of bright green morays.

DIVE SITES ON THE EAST SIDE
CAPTAIN ROGER WRECK. A plethora of colorful fish swish about this old tugboat, which rests off the coast at Seroe Colorado. From shore you can swim to a steep coral reef nearby.

ISLA DI ORO. A wide expanse of reef grows far out along the shallow bank, making for superb diving. You'll be treated to views of green moray eels, coral crabs, trumpet fish, and French, gray, and queen angelfish.

JANE WRECK. This 200-ft freighter, lodged in an almost vertical position at a depth of 90 ft, is near the coral reef west of Palm Island. Night diving is exciting here, as the polyps emerge from the corals that grow profusely on the steel plates of the decks and cabins. Soft corals and sea fans are also abundant in the area.

PALM ISLAND. Secluded behind clusters of mangrove, the reef system around Palm Island stretches all the way to Oranjestad. You can get close enough to touch the nurse sharks that sleep tucked into reef crevices during the day.

PUNTA BASORA. This narrow reef stretches far into the sea off the island's easternmost point. On calm days you'll see eagle rays, stingrays, barracudas, and hammerhead sharks, as well as hawksbill and loggerhead turtles.

SHARK CAVES. At this site along the island's southeastern point you can swim alongside sand sharks and float past the nurse sharks sleeping under the rock outcroppings.

VERA WRECK. In 1954, this freighter sank while en route to North America. The crewmen, who were saved by an Aruban captain, claimed that the cargo consisted of Nazi treasures.

THE WALL. From May to August, green sea turtles intent on laying their eggs abound at this steep-walled reef. You'll also spot long-branched gorgons, groupers, and burrfish swimming nearby. Close to shore, massive sheet corals are plentiful; in the upper part of the reef are colorful varieties like black coral, star coral, and flower coral. Flitting about are brilliant damselfish, rock beauties, and porgies.

Skydiving

You can fall head over heels for Aruba as you leap out of an airplane at 10,000 ft. Tandem jumps are offered early in the morning seven days a week by **SKYDIVE ARUBA** (Paradera 211,

Yani Brokke: Olympic Athlete

"I like sports, and they like me, too," says the multitalented athlete Yani Brokke. "I can try a sport for the first time and in two days I can play." The 71-year-old Aruban, who started playing soccer at age 7, has since represented the island in Olympic basketball, tennis, baseball, and soccer. He has played in packed stadiums, received merits and ribbons from the government, and has been decorated with medals by Queen Beatrix herself.

"In the old days, there wasn't much to do on Aruba," says Brokke, who still gives tennis lessons at the Bushiri Hotel every weekday afternoon. "Life was all about school and sports. Today, kids are involved in computers, TV, sports, and parties as well as other distractions." Despite his success, the often self-coached Brokke believes he was born too early. "There was a lot of good talent but a lack of guidance, and aspiring athletes needed people to back them up. These days, good players get coaches and have a little more direction."

Paradera, tel. 297/8–35067 or 297/9–37151). To make the leap, you must be over 18 years old, under 240 pounds, and in good health. This remarkable two-hour experience costs $220.

Tennis

Aruba's winds make tennis a challenge even if you have the best of backhands. Although visitors can make arrangements to play at the resorts, priority goes to guests. Some private tennis clubs can also accommodate you. Try the world-class facilities at the **ARUBA RACQUET CLUB** (Rooisanto 21, Palm Beach, tel. 297/8–60215). Host to a variety of international tournaments, the club has eight courts (six lighted), as well as a swimming pool, an aerobics center, and a restaurant. Fees are $10 per hour; a lesson with a pro costs $20 for a half hour, $35 for one hour.

Windsurfing

Whisk through the waves and revel in the sea spray. Aruba has all it takes for windsurfing: trade winds that average 15 knots year-round (peaking May–July); a sunny climate; and picture-perfect azure blue waters. With a few lessons from a certified instructor, even novices will be jibing in no time. The southwestern coast's tranquil waters make it ideal for both beginners and intermediates, as the winds are steady but sudden gusts rare. Experts will find the waters of the Atlantic, especially around Grapefield and Boca Grandi beaches, more challenging; winds are fierce and often shift without warning. Rentals average about $60 a day, and lessons range from $45 to $75. Many hotels include windsurfing in their water sports packages, and most operators can help you arrange complete windsurfing vacations.

Every June sees the Aruba Hi-Winds competition, with professional and amateur windsurfers from around the world. There are divisions for women, men, juniors, masters, and grand masters. Disciplines include slalom, course racing, long distance, and free-style. The entry fee is $150 (there's a $25 discount if you register on-line at www.aruba-hiwinds.com).

ARUBA BEACH VILLAS (L. G. Smith Blvd. 462, Malmok Beach, tel. 297/8–62527; 800/320–9998 in the U.S., www.arubasailboardvacations.com) offers first-rate instruction. It's at Windsurf Village, a lodging complex created by and for windsurfers near Fisherman's Huts, a world-renowned sailing spot. Another lure for those in the know: the complex is home to one of the Caribbean's largest and best-stocked windsurfing shops.

FISHERMAN'S HUTS WINDSURF CENTER (Aruba Marriott Resort, L. G. Smith Blvd. 101, Palm Beach, tel. 297/8–69898) is a popular spot among wanna-be and expert windsurfers alike. **PELICAN TOURS & WATERSPORTS** (J. E. Irausquin Blvd. 232,

Palm Beach, tel. 297/8–72302, www.pelican-aruba.com) usually has boards and sails on hand. **ROGER'S WINDSURF PLACE** (L. G. Smith Blvd. 472, Malmok Beach, tel. 297/8–61918, www. rogerswindsurf.com) is located where the winds carry fastest over calmer waters. The day will fly by when you windsurf with **SAILBOARD VACATIONS** (L. G. Smith Blvd. 462, Malmok Beach, tel. 297/8–61072, www.sailboardvacations.com). Trade jokes and snap photos with your fellow windsurfers at **VELA ARUBA** (Palm Beach, tel. 297/8–69000 ext. 6430, www.velawindsurf. com). This is the place to make friends on the water.

Hooiberg loomed before the adventure-seeker. Water bottle in hand, he gingerly began his ascent. His breath grew shorter as he made his way up. Within 15 minutes he reached the top and paused to take in a view that stretched all the way to Venezuela. Leonardo DeCaprio's line in Titanic flashed through his mind: "I'm the king of the world!" On the way down, he encountered a group about to embark on the same journey. "Piece of cake," he offered, nodding toward the hill. Then he headed back to his hotel for a massage.

In This Chapter

here and there

ARUBA'S WILDLY SCULPTED LANDSCAPE is replete with rocky deserts, cactus clusters, secluded coves, blue vistas, and the trademark divi-divi tree. To preserve the environment while encouraging visitors to explore, the government has implemented the first phases of a 10-year, $10 million ecotourism plan. Initiatives include finding ways to make efficient use of the limited land resources and protecting the natural and cultural resources in such preserves as Arikok National Park and the Coastal Protection Zone (along the island's north and east coasts).

Oranjestad, Aruba's capital, is good for shopping by day and dining by night, but the "real Aruba"—with its untamed beauty—can be found only in the countryside. Rent a car, take a sightseeing tour, or hire a cab for $30 an hour. Though desolate, the northern and eastern shores are striking and well worth a visit. A drive out past the California Lighthouse or to Seroe Colorado will give you a feel for the backcountry.

Although the main highways are well paved, the windward side of the island still has some roads that are a mixture of compacted dirt and stones. A car is fine, but a four-wheel-drive vehicle will enable you to better navigate the unpaved interior. Remember that few beaches outside the hotel strip along Palm and Eagle beaches to the west have refreshment stands, so pack your own food and drink. Aside from those in the infrequent restaurant, there are no public bathrooms outside of Oranjestad.

Traffic is sparse, but signs leading to sights are often small and hand-lettered (this is slowly changing as the government puts up official road signs), so watch closely. Route 1A travels southbound along the western coast, and 1B is simply northbound along the same road. If you lose your way, just follow the divi-divi trees.

Numbers in the margin correspond to points of interest on the Exploring map.

WESTERN ARUBA

Western Aruba is where you'll spend most of your time. All the resorts and time-shares are along this coast, most of them clustered on the oceanfront strip at the luscious Palm and Eagle beaches, in the city of Oranjestad, or in the district of Noord. All the casinos, major shopping malls, and most restaurants are found in this region, as is the airport.

A Good Tour

Rent a car and head out on Route 1A toward **ORANJESTAD** ① for a couple of hours of sightseeing and shopping. Then drive inland along Route 6A, passing the town of Paradera. Pick up Route 4A and follow it a short way to the **AYO AND CASIBARI ROCK FORMATIONS** ②. Continue on 4A and follow the signs for **HOOIBERG** ③; if you're so inclined, climb the steps of Haystack Hill for an outrageous view. Return to 6A and drive a couple of miles to the Bushiribana Gold Smelter. Beyond it on the windward coast is the **NATURAL BRIDGE** ④. You'll have to veer off 6A, which bends east here; follow the signs.

Retrace your drive to Route 6; take 6B to the intersection of Route 3B, which you'll follow into the town of **NOORD** ⑤, a good place to stop for lunch. Then take Route 2B, following the signs for the branch road to the **ALTO VISTA CHAPEL** ⑥. Return to town and pick up 2B and then 1B to reach the **CALIFORNIA LIGHTHOUSE** ⑦. In this area you'll also see Arashi Beach (a popular snorkeling site) and the Tierra Del Sol golf course. From the lighthouse follow 1A back toward Palm Beach. On the way, stop at the **BUTTERFLY FARM** ⑧, **DE OLDE MOLEN** ⑨, and the **BUBALI BIRD SANCTUARY** ⑩.

TIMING
If you head out right after breakfast, you can just about complete the tour above in one very full day. If you want to linger in Oranjestad's shops or you want to go snorkeling along the beach, consider breaking the tour up into two days.

What to See

⑥ **ALTO VISTA CHAPEL.** On the island's northwest corner, amid eerie boulders and looming cacti, sits the scenic little Alto Vista Chapel. The wind whistles through the simple mustard-color walls. Along the side of the road back to civilization are miniature crosses with depictions of the stations of the cross and hand-lettered signs exhorting PRAY FOR US, SINNERS and the like—a simple yet powerful evocation of faith. To get here, follow the rough, winding dirt road that loops around the island's northern tip. From the hotel strip, take Palm Beach Road through three intersections and watch for the asphalt road to the left just past the Alto Vista Rum Shop.

② **AYO AND CASIBARI ROCK FORMATIONS.** The massive boulders at Ayo and Casibari are a mystery, as they don't match the island's geological makeup. You can climb to the top for fine views of the arid countryside. On the way you'll doubtless pass Aruba whiptail lizards—the males are cobalt blue, the females blue with dots. The main path to Casibari has steps and handrails (except on one side), and you must move through tunnels and along narrow steps and ledges to reach the top. At Ayo you'll find ancient pictographs in a small cave (the entrance has iron bars to protect the drawings from vandalism). You may also encounter a boulder climber, one of many adventurers who are increasingly drawn to Ayo's smooth surfaces. Access to Casibari is via Tanki Highway 4A to Ayo via Route

exploring

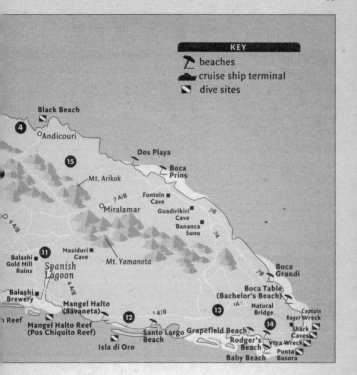

KEY

beaches

cruise ship terminal

dive sites

Black Beach

4

Andicouri

15

Mt. Arikok

Dos Playa

Boca Prins

Fontein Cave

7 A/B

Miralamar

Guadirikiri Cave

Bananca Sunu

7B

7A

O 4 A/B

Masiduri Cave

Balashi Gold Mill Ruins

11

Spanish Lagoon

Mt. Yamanota

4 A/B

Boca Grandi

7B

Boca Table (Bachelor's Beach)

Balashi Brewery

Mangel Halto (Savaneta)

Natural Bridge

1A

Captain Roger Wreck

n Reef

12

1 A/B

13

Mangel Halto Reef (Pos Chiquito Reef)

Santo Largo Beach

Grapefield Beach

14

Shark Caves

Isla di Oro

Rodger's Beach

Vera Wreck

Punta Basora

Baby Beach

6A; watch carefully for the turnoff signs near the center of the island on the way to the windward side.

⑩ BUBALI BIRD SANCTUARY. Bird-watchers delight in the more than 80 species of migratory birds that nest in this wetlands area inland from the island's strip of high-rise hotels. Herons, egrets, cormorants, coots, gulls, skimmers, terns, and ducks are among the winged wonders in and around the two interconnected man-made lakes that compose the sanctuary. *J. E. Irausqin Blvd., Noord, no phone. Free.*

⑧ BUTTERFLY FARM. Hundreds of butterflies from around the world flutter by at this spectacular garden. Guided 20- to 30-minute tours (included in the price of admission) provide an entertaining look into how these creatures complete their life cycle: from egg to caterpillar to chrysalis to butterfly. After your initial visit, you can return as often as you like for free. *J. E. Irausqin Blvd., Palm Beach, tel. 297/8–63656, www.thebutterflyfarm.com. $10. Daily 9–4:30 (last tour at 4).*

⑦ CALIFORNIA LIGHTHOUSE. This lighthouse, built by a French architect in 1910, stands at the island's far northern end. Although the interior is closed to the public, you can ascend the hill to its base for some great views. In this stark landscape you'll feel as though you've just landed on the moon. The structure is surrounded by huge boulders that look like extraterrestrial monsters and sand dunes embroidered with scrub that resemble undulating sea serpents. Next to the nearby Trattoria El Farro Blanco—a great place to watch the sun set—there's a placard explaining the lighthouse's history and telling of the wreck of a German ship just offshore.

③ HOOIBERG. Named for its unusual shape (*hooiberg* means "haystack" in Dutch), this 541-ft peak lies inland just past the airport. Climb the 562 steps to the top for an impressive view of the city of Oranjestad. On a clear day, you can even see the northern coast of Venezuela.

The Divi-Divi Tree

Like a statuesque dancer in a graceful flat-back pose, the watapana, or divi-divi tree, is one of Aruba's hallmarks. Oddly enough, this tropical shrub is a member of the legume family. Its astringent pods contain high levels of tannin, which is leached out for tanning leather. The pods also yield a black dye. The tree has a moderate rate of growth and a high drought tolerance. Typically it reaches no more than 25 ft in height, with a flattened crown and irregular, forked branches. Its leaves are dull green, and its inconspicuous yet fragrant flowers are pale yellow or white and grow in small clusters. Thanks to constant trade winds, the divi-divis serve as a natural compass: they're bent toward the island's leeward, or western, side where most of the hotels are.

④ **NATURAL BRIDGE.** Centuries of raging tides sculpted this coral rock bridge in the center of the windward coast. To reach it, drive inland along Hospitalstraat and then follow the signs. Just before you reach the geological wonder you'll pass the massive stone ruins of the Bushiribana Gold Smelter, an intriguing structure that resembles a crumbling fortress, and a section of surf-pounded coastline called Boca Mahos. Near Natural Bridge are a souvenir shop and a café overlooking the water.

⑤ **NOORD.** The district of Noord is home to the strip of high-rise hotels and casinos that line Palm Beach. Here you'll also find the beautiful St. Ann's Church, known for its ornate 19th century altar. In this area, Aruban-style homes are scattered amid clusters of cacti.

9 DE OLDE MOLEN. This windmill dates from 1804, when it was built in the Dutch town of Friesland to pump water out of land that lay below sea level. Damaged by a storm in 1878, it was taken apart and then reconstructed in another town, where it was used to mill grains. After another brutal storm in 1929 it remained idle until 1960, when a Dutch merchant purchased its wooden frame. It was shipped piece by piece to Aruba and rebuilt atop a two-story concrete structure in 1974. It now houses a museum—containing Dutch antiques, local farming implements, and a traditional horse-and-carriage display—and the Mill Restaurant, which serves fresh local seafood, beef, chicken, veal, and a special Dutch pea soup. A bar at the museum is open until just before midnight, so you can party at this unique setting. *L. G. Smith Blvd. 330, Noord, tel. 297/8–66300 or 297/8–62060. Free.*

1 ORANJESTAD. Aruba's charming capital is best explored on foot. Its palm-lined central thoroughfare runs between old and new pastel-painted buildings of typical Dutch design (Spanish influence is also evident in some of the architecture). There are many malls with boutiques and shops; downtown and Seaport Village are the major shopping areas. Every morning, the wharf teems with activity as merchants sell produce and fresh fish—often right off their boats. You can also buy handicrafts and T-shirts at this dockside bazaar, where bargaining is expected and dollars or florins are accepted. Island schooners and houseboats anchored near the fishing boats add to the port's ambience. Wilhelmina Park, a small tropical garden on the waterfront along L. G. Smith Boulevard, has a sculpture of the Netherlands' Queen Wilhelmina, whose reign lasted from 1890 to 1948.

At the **Archaeological Museum of Aruba** you'll find two rooms chock-full of fascinating artifacts from indigenous peoples, farm and domestic utensils, and skeletons. *J. E. Irausquinplein 2A, tel. 297/8–28979. Free. Weekdays 8–noon and 1–4.*

One of the island's oldest edifices, **Fort Zoutman** was built in 1796 and played an important role in skirmishes between British and

Curaçao troops in 1803. The Willem III Tower, named for the Dutch monarch of that time, was added in 1868 to serve as a lighthouse. Over time, the fort has been put to use as a government office building, a police station, and a prison. Now its historical museum displays Aruban artifacts in an 18th-century house. *Zoutmanstraat, tel. 297/8–26099. Free. Weekdays 8–noon and 1–4.*

The tiny **Numismatic Museum of Aruba,** next to St. Francis Roman Catholic Church, displays a host of currencies—including a few salvaged from shipwrecks in the region. Some of the coins on display circulated during the Roman Empire, the Byzantine Empire, and the ancient Chinese dynasties; a few date as far back as the 5th century BC. The museum had its start as one Aruban's private collection and is now run by a family. *Zuidstraat 7, tel. 297/8–28831. Free. Weekdays 7:30–noon and 1–4:30.*

Built in 1962, **Beth Israel Synagogue** is the only Jewish house of worship on Aruba, and it strives to meet the needs of its Ashkenazi, Sephardic, European, North American, and South American worshipers. The island's Jewish community dates back to the opening of the oil refinery in the 1920s, when small congregations met in private homes in San Nicolas. The temple holds regular services on Friday at 8 PM—followed by a kiddush—and on Saturday at 8 AM; additional services are held on high holy days. Visitors are always welcome, although it's best to make an appointment to see the synagogue when there's not a service. A Judaica shop sells keepsakes; at press time, there were plans to add kosher dry goods and kiddush wines to the stock. *Adrian Laclé Blvd. 2, tel. 297/8–23272. Free except high holy days, when tickets are required.*

EASTERN ARUBA

In addition to the vast Arikok National Park, eastern Aruba is home to the island's second largest city, San Nicolas, and several charming fishing villages and pristine beaches. Here you'll get a real sense of traditional island life.

A Good Tour

Take Route 1A to Route 4B and visit the Balashi Gold Smelter ruins and **FRENCHMAN'S PASS** ⑪. Return to 1A and continue your drive past Mangel Halto Beach to **SAVANETA** ⑫, a fishing village and one of several residential areas that has examples of typical Aruban homes. Follow 1A to **SAN NICOLAS** ⑬, where you can meander along the main promenade, pick up a few souvenirs, and grab a bite to eat. Heading out of town, continue on 1A until you hit a fork in the road; follow the signs toward **SEROE COLORADO** ⑭, with the nearby natural bridge and the Colorado Point Lighthouse. From here, follow the signs toward Rodgers Beach, just one of several area shores where you can kick back for a while. Nearby Baby Beach, with calm waters and beautiful white sand, is a favorite spot for snorkelers. To the north, on Route 7B, is Boca Grandi, a great windsurfing spot. Next is Grapefield Beach, a stretch of glistening white sand against a backdrop of cliffs and boulder formations. Shortly beyond it, on 7B, you'll come into **ARIKOK NATIONAL PARK** ⑮, where you can explore caves and tunnels, play on sand dunes, and tackle Mt. Yamanota, Aruba's highest elevation. Farther along 7B is Santa Cruz, where a wooden cross stands atop a hill to mark the spot where Christianity was introduced to the islanders. The same highway will bring you all the way into Oranjestad.

TIMING

You can follow the tour and see many of the sights in a half day, though it's easy to fill a full day if you spend time relaxing on a sandy beach or exploring the trails in Arikok National Park.

What to See

⑮ **ARIKOK NATIONAL PARK.** Nearly 20% of Aruba has been designated part of this national park, the keystone of the government's long-term ecotourism plan. Most of it sprawls across the interior, stretching to the north and encompassing a long strip of the windward shoreline. Within the confines of the park, near the island's center, is Mt. Arikok, the heart of a natural preserve that showcases the island's flora and fauna, the ruins of a gold-mining operation at Miralmar, and the remnants of Dutch peasant settlements at Masiduri. The 620-ft Mt. Yamanota, Aruba's highest peak, is also in the park.

Anyone looking for geological exotica should head for the park's caves, found on the northeastern coast. Baranca Sunu, the so-called Tunnel of Love, has a heart-shape entrance and naturally sculpted rocks farther inside that look like the Madonna, Abe Lincoln, and even a jaguar. Guadirikiri Cave and Fontein Cave are marked with ancient drawings (rangers are on hand to offer explanations), as both were used by indigenous people centuries ago. Bats are known to make appearances—don't worry, they won't bother you. Although you don't need a flashlight because the paths are well lighted, it's best to wear sneakers.

⓫ **FRENCHMAN'S PASS.** Overhanging trees and towering cacti border this luscious stretch of road. The pass is almost midway between Oranjestad and San Nicolas; follow L. G. Smith Boulevard past a shimmering vista of blue-green sea and turn off where you see the drive-in theater (a popular local hangout). Then drive to the first intersection, turn right, and follow the curve to the right. Gold was discovered on Aruba in 1824, and near Frenchman's Pass are the massive cement-and-limestone ruins of the **Balashi Gold Smelter,** a lovely place to picnic and listen to the parakeets. A magnificent, gnarled divi-divi tree guards the entrance. The area now is home to Aruba's desalination plant, where all of the island's drinking water is produced.

⓭ **SAN NICOLAS.** During the heyday of the oil refineries, Aruba's oldest village was a bustling port; now it's primary purpose is tourism. The main promenade is full of interesting kiosks, and the whole district is undergoing a revitalization project that will bring parks, a cultural center, a central market, a public swimming pool, and an arts promenade. The institution in town is Charlie's

Cunucu Houses

Pastel houses surrounded by cacti fences adorn Aruba's flat, rugged cunucu ("country" in Papiamento). The features of these traditional houses were developed in response to the environment. Early settlers discovered that slanting roofs allowed the heat to rise and that small windows helped to keep in the cool air. Among the earliest building materials was caliche, a durable calcium carbonate substance found in the island's southeastern hills. Many houses were also built using interlocking coral rocks that didn't require mortar (this technique is no longer used, thanks to cement and concrete). Contemporary design combines some of the basic principles of the earlier homes with touches of modernization: windows, though still narrow, have been elongated; roofs are constructed of bright tiles; pretty patios have been added; and doorways and balconies present an ornamental face to the world beyond.

Restaurant & Bar, a hangout for more than 50 years. Stop in for a drink and advice on what to see and do in this little town.

⓬ **SAVANETA.** The Dutch settled here after retaking the island in 1816, and it served as Aruba's first capital. Today it's a bustling fishing village with a 150-year-old *cas de torto* (mud hut), the oldest house still standing on the island.

⓮ **SEROE COLORADO.** What was originally built as a community for oil workers is known for its intriguing 1939 chapel. The site is surreal, as organ pipe cacti—nearly as tall as the refinery's belching smokestacks—form the backdrop for sedate whitewashed cottages. The real reason to come here is a second **natural bridge,** this one less well-known. Keep bearing east past the community, continuing uphill until you run out of road. You can then hike down to the cathedral-like formation. It's not too strenuous, but watch your footing as you descend. Be sure to follow the white arrows painted on the rocks, as there are no other directional signs. Although this bridge isn't as spectacular as its more celebrated sibling, the raw elemental power of the sea that created it, replete with hissing blow holes, certainly is.

There's a traffic jam on L. G. Smith Boulevard—it's 11 PM on Friday and everyone is trying to get into Oranjestad. A cab pulls into the Havana Club parking lot, weaving through swarms of scantily clad women and casually dressed men. The pulse of Oreo, the island's most famous band, and an air of anticipation grip the nightcrawlers waiting to get in. Only when the oversize door swings open does the night really begin.

In this Chapter

nightlife

THEY PUMP UP THE VOLUME at Aruba's resort bars when the sun sets. Unlike many other islands, nightlife here isn't confined to touristy folkloric shows. In addition to spending time in one of the many casinos, you can slowly savor a drink while the sun dips into the sea, dance to the beat of a local band, bar-hop in a colorful bus, or simply stroll along a deserted starlit beach.

HOW AND WHEN

Arubans like to party—the more the merrier—and they usually start celebrating late in the evening. The action, mostly on weekends, doesn't pick up until around midnight. Casual yet trendy attire is the norm. Most bars don't have a cover charge, although most nightclubs do. Bigger clubs, such as E-Zone, have lines on weekends, but they move quickly; use this time to start your socializing and you may just end up with a dance partner before you even step foot inside the door. Drink specials are available at some bars, and every establishment will gladly give you a free Balashi Cocktail (the local term for a glass of water). Both bars and clubs have either live bands or DJs depending on the night.

No matter where you choose to party, be smart about getting back to your hotel. Drinking and driving is against the law. If you're within walking distance, go ahead and hoof it. Taxis are a good option if your hotel is farther away. The island is safe, and you'll probably wander with swarms of other visitors in town and along Palm Beach.

A Bartender's Life

Albert Tromp has been mixing drinks in the bars and restaurants of Aruba for more than 30 years. He started out as a barback at the Aruba Caribbean, then worked for the Manchebo Beach Hotel, the Sheraton, and the Americana, where he served as head bartender for six years. Tromp also ran his own restaurant for 2½ years, but decided to return to the bartending life. He's now the beverage manager at the Radisson—where the glassware is oversize, the cocktails are creative, and the wine list is extensive.

Tromp is well-known on Aruba, having served up drinks to so many guests. He's rubbed elbows with celebrities, including actor Chuck Norris and musician Kenny G. Tromp also had a visit from Sinbad (he drank Seagram's and water, while his crew put down lots of Jack Daniels). The comedian, who was filming a movie in Venezuela, flew to Aruba for the weekend with about 2,000 of his closest friends.

Tastes have changed over the years, according to Tromp. "In the '70s," he says, "I sold tons of martinis." Drinks with exotic names and flavors seem to be in favor now. Folks come from everywhere, for example, to sample his famous Albert Special (also known as the Key Banana Blast), a combination of local liquors like rum, crème de banana, and coconut-flavored poncha crema with blue Curaçao poured in the bottom and down the sides. If you overindulge, ask Tromp to prepare you one of his secret hangover curatives.

Tromp has organized competitions, such as the Aruba Bartender's Contest that searches for the summer's best cocktail. He also helped to define the taste of Balashi—the island's first local brew—by sitting on the panel that conducted tastings for color, foam, and flavor. Tromp says he's proud to serve the hometown favorite. "Tourists would always come to the bar and ask to try the local beer," he says, "and we would serve Amstel, which is brewed on Curaçao, since that was the closest thing we had."

SOURCES

For information on specific events check out the free magazines *Aruba Nights*, *Aruba Events*, *Aruba Experience*, and *Aruba Holiday*, all available at the airport and at hotels.

Bar-Hopping Buses

A couple of bus operators can turn a regular evening out on the town into a whirlwind tour of the island's hottest nightspots. One uniquely Aruban institution is a psychedelically painted '57 Chevy bus called the *KUKOO KUNUKU* (tel. 297/8–62010). Weeknights you'll find as many as 40 passengers traveling between six bars from sundown to around midnight. The $55 fee per passenger includes dinner, drinks, and picking you up (and pouring you off) at your hotel. Group and private charter rates are available. Needless to say, reservations are essential.

Bars

Catch a glimpse of the elaborate swimming pool with whirlpools, waterslides, and waterfalls from the Hyatt Regency Aruba Beach Resort & Casino's **ALFRESCO LOBBY BAR** (J. E. Irausquin Blvd. 85, Palm Beach, tel. 297/8–61234 ext. 4265) while sipping premium wine or a tropical cocktail. This is where guests gather to hear live music early in the evening and stop by for a nightcap after the casino closes. Many visitors, including those on party buses, find their way to **CARLOS & CHARLIE'S** (Weststraat 3A, Oranjestad, tel. 297/8–20355), which may be why locals shy away from it. You'll find mixed drinks by the yard, Mexican fare, and American music from the '60s, '70s, and '80s. Set in a former fisherman's house behind Royal Plaza Mall is **CASTAWAY'S** (Schelpstraat 43, Oranjestad, tel. 297/8–33606), a popular restaurant and bar. The beer is cold, the service is cheerful, and the all-you-can-eat ribs are famous around the island.

Brewing Up Something Special

There was a time when you could walk into any bar in Aruba and get a glass of water by asking for a "Balashi Cocktail." (The name came from the fact that the desalination plant is located in an area known as Balashi.) Since the creation of Balashi, the first locally brewed beer, such a drink order now has a whole new meaning. Made by a German brewmaster in a state-of-the-art facility using only the finest hops and malt, Balashi is golden-colored pilsner.

Balashi is a source of local pride, even more so now that it won the prestigious "Monde Selection" at an international competition in 2001. Visitors love it as well. "It's a big tourist thing," explains Gerben Tilma, general manager of the plant. "Everyone wants to know what the best local products are. Now we can tell them."

The **BALASHI BREWERY** (Balashi, tel. 297/8–54805) has free 30-minute tours that begin every half hour between 10 AM and 2 PM daily. There's also a souvenir shop, a café, and a 10,000-square-ft beer garden where you can enjoy a cold one.

In business since 1948, **CHETA'S BAR** (Paradera 119, Paradera, tel. 297/8–23689) is a real local joint that holds no more than four customers at a time. There aren't any bar stools, either, which is why most patrons gather out front. During the Saturday-afternoon happy hour, people mingle in the street and lean on their cars while sipping a cold Balashi ($1.35) and munching on buns from Bright Bakery. No one even seems to mind that the bar's lack of a liquor license means it can't serve mixed drinks and that it must close by 9 PM (it opens at 8:30 AM, though). Drive into Seroe Colorado, on the far side of Rodger's Beach, and you'll see a two-level structure overlooking the crystal-clear blue bay. **COCO BEACH BAR & RESTAURANT** (Rodger's Beach, Seroe Colorado, tel. 297/8–43434) is a popular spot for food and drinks day or evening.

GALLEY BAR & LOUNGE (La Cabana All Suite Beach Resort & Casino, J. E. Irausquin Blvd. 250, Eagle Beach, tel. 297/8–79000) serves late-afternoon and evening cocktails. **IGUANA JOE'S** (Royal Plaza Mall, L. G. Smith Blvd. 94, Oranjestad, tel. 297/8–39373) has a creative reptilian-theme decor and a color scheme featuring such planter's-punch shades as lime and grape.

JIMMY'S PLACE (Kruisweg 15, Oranjestad, tel. 297/8–22550) is a smoky joint that attracts all types, from bankers and lawyers to the staff from other bars. Happy hour on Friday is a good time to stop by, sip a cocktail, smoke a stogie, and unwind. The after-hours crowd often turns up here for late-night soups and sandwiches. The laid-back beachfront **KOKOA** (Palm Beach, tel. 297/8–62050) is often full of beauties in skimpy bathing suits and windsurfer guys in shorts. It's a popular spot on Sunday and Tuesday, which are reggae nights.

With parrots painted on the ceiling, **MAMBO JAMBO** (Royal Plaza Mall, 2nd fl., L. G. Smith Blvd. 94, Oranjestad, tel. 297/8–33632) is daubed in sunset colors. Sip one of several unique libations sold nowhere else, or browse for Mambo Jambo memorabilia at a shop next door. With front-row seats to view the green flash—that ray of light that flicks through the sky as the sun sinks into the ocean—the **PALMS BAR** (Hyatt Regency Aruba Beach Resort & Casino, J. E. Irausquin Blvd. 85, Palm Beach, tel. 297/8–61234) is the perfect spot to enjoy the sunset.

The atmosphere at **SALT & PEPPER** (J. E. Irausquin Blvd. 370A, Palm Beach, tel. 297/8–63280) is a mixture of Dutch and Latin American. Come for the wide variety of tapas and the good selection of reasonably priced Chilean wines.

Cruises

On the **SALTY DOG SUNSET CRUISE** (tel. 297/8–62010), aboard the 80-ft sailing vessel dubbed *Mi Dushi*, you can enjoy Caribbean snacks as you toast with champagne. The open-air bar makes a nice place to meet fellow travelers. Cruises depart Wednesdays and Fridays at 5 PM from the Aruba Grand Beach Resort Pier and return about 7 PM. The cost is $35 per person.

Don't be surprised if you're enjoying a romantic ocean-view dinner on Palm Beach and you see a twinkle of lights on the horizon. It may be the *TATTOO* (tel. 297/8–62010), a catamaran that sails every night except Sunday from 8 PM to midnight. It has three decks for dancing (there are live bands and a DJ), dining, and star-gazing. End the evening with the famous Tattoo rope swing and water slide. The $49 fee includes dinner.

Dance and Music Clubs

The **BUSHIRI BEACH RESORT POOL BAR** (L. G. Smith Blvd. 35, Punta Brabo, tel. 297/8–25216) isn't just for lounging. On Friday night, a group of talented teenagers called the Popcorn Dancers performs at 9 PM. Any other night, stop by for live music between 7 and 11. At **CAFÉ BAHIA** (Weststraat 7, Oranjestad, tel. 297/8–89982) an elegant spiral staircase leads up to a bar and dance floor backed by a mural of colorful cacti against a cloud-smattered Aruban sky. Locals and tourists drink cocktails and sashay to salsa music provided by island bands.

Live bands perform at the **CELLAR** (Klipstraat 2, Oranjestad, tel. 297/8–26490) Monday and Thursday to Saturday. The music du jour might be blues, jazz, funk, reggae, or rock. Bartenders in hard hats serve up drinks at the exotic **E-ZONE** (Bayside Mall, Westraat 5, Oranjestad, tel. 297/8–87474), where the walls are decorated with hair-dryer tubes and other oddities. The huge stainless-steel dance floor doesn't fill up till after 1 AM. The crowd—always eager to hear a local band called Crystal Breeze—is best described as eclectic. There's a $5 cover charge.

The energy doesn't diminish until closing time at **CLUB 2000** (Royal Plaza Mall, 2nd fl., L. G. Smith Blvd. 82, Oranjestad, tel. 297/8–38842), owing to a young crowd that lives for American

Cool Concoctions

These drink recipes come from Aruban-born bartender Clive Van Der Linde.

THE WOW. Mix equal parts (2 ounces or so) of rum and vodka as well as triple sec, a splash of tequila, grenadine, coconut cream, and pineapple and orange juice. Quips Van Der Linde, "You won't taste the alcohol, but after two, you'll feel pretty good."

THE IGUANA. Mix equal parts of rum, vodka, and add either blue Curaçao or blue grenadine for color. Add crème de banana liqueur, coconut cream, and pineapple juice. Says Van Der Linde, "I learned this one more than 10 years ago on the first sailing boat I worked on. It was called the Balia, which means 'to dance.' "

THE CAPTAIN'S SPECIAL. Mix equal parts of rum and vodka, and add a splash of amaretto, crème de banana, and pineapple and orange juice. "It's really simple," says Van Der Linde. "Just blend with crushed ice and it's ready to drink."

rap music. The dance floor and circular bar throb to the movement of the crowds. The cover charge is $5. **LA FIESTA** (Aventura Mall, Plaza Daniel Leo, Oranjestad, tel. 297/8–35896), an upscale bar with indoor and outdoor spaces, attracts a casual yet classy crowd. A couple of laps around the wraparound terrace overlooking the main street gives night owls a chance to scope out the black-clad crowd. Inside, heavy red curtains add drama. Although there's no dance floor, a cool mix of music inspires patrons to bop at the bar.

Stop by the cozy **SIROCCO LOUNGE** (Wyndham Aruba Beach Resort & Casino, L. G. Smith Blvd. 77, Palm Beach, tel. 297/8–64466) for jazz performances Thursday through Saturday. For jazz and other types of music, try the **GARUFA CIGAR & COCKTAIL LOUNGE** (Wilhelminastraat 63, Oranjestad, tel. 297/

8–27205), a cozy cigar bar. It serves as a lounge for customers awaiting a table at the nearby El Gaucho Argentine Grill (you're issued a beeper so you know when your table is ready). While you wait, have a drink, enjoy some appetizers, and take in the leopard-print carpet and funky bar stools. The ambience may draw you back for an after-dinner cognac.

Local bands are always in the spotlight at the beach-side **GILLIGAN'S** (Radisson Aruba Caribbean Resort, J. E. Irausquin Blvd. 81, Palm Beach, tel. 297/8–66555). You'll feel like you've been shipwrecked on an uncharted tropic isle as you sip drinks at the bar. Friday and Saturday night you can catch Supermania, one of Aruba's most celebrated bands, at **PATA PATA** (La Cabana All Suite Beach Resort & Casino, J. E. Irausquin Blvd. 250, Eagle Beach, tel. 297/8–79000). Live music nightly makes **PELICAN TERRACE** (Divi Aruba Beach Resort, J. E. Irausquin Blvd. 45 Manchebo Beach, tel. 297/8–23300) a popular nightspot. Sip creative cocktails, dance around the pool, and grab a late-night snack—perhaps a pizza hot from the wood-burning oven.

Local bands alternate sets at **RICK'S CAFÉ AMERICAN** (Wyndham Aruba Beach Resort & Casino, J. E. Irausquin Blvd. 77, Palm Beach, tel. 297/8–64466), where fruity cocktails and refreshing beers are always available. As the bar is in the hotel's casino, you can throw a quarter in the slots on your way in—you just might win enough to cover your bar tab. At the **STELLARIS LOUNGE & LOBBY BAR** (Aruba Marriott Resort & Stellaris Casino, L. G. Smith Blvd. 101, Palm Beach, tel. 297/8–69000) nightly entertainment is provided by a local band that gets the party started at about 9 PM and keeps it going till at least 2 AM.

Movies

The **SEAPORT CINEMA** (Seaport Market Place, tel. 297/8–30318) has six theaters showing the latest American movies. The earliest shows are around 4 PM; late shows start around 10:30 PM. Ticket prices range from $5.50 to $7.

Check out the not-so-silver screen under the stars at the **E. DE VEER DRIVE-IN THEATER** (Kibaima, tel. 297/8–58355). It will cost you about $3 to watch the English-language movies on this massive screen in a field near Balashi. Movies start at 8:30 PM. The drive-in can accommodate about 100 cars and has a snack bar.

Theme Nights

At last count there were more than 50 theme nights offered during the course of a week. Each "party" features a buffet dinner, dancing, and entertainment (often of the limbo, steel-band, stilt-walking variety). The top groups tend to rotate among the resorts. For a complete list contact the Aruba Tourism Authority. One of the best bets is the **HAVANA TROPICAL** (Wyndham Aruba Beach Resort & Casino, J. E. Irausquin Blvd. 77, Palm Beach, tel. 297/8–64466), which has parties every night except Wednesday and Sunday. The **CARIBBEAN CARNIVAL NIGHT** (Aruba Sonesta Resorts at Seaport Village, L. G. Smith Blvd. 9, Oranjestad, tel. 297/8–36000) shines on Monday.

It's Tuesday night at the Bon Bini Festival. Performers run onto the stage as steel-pan drummers pound out a heart-racing beat. The rhythm prompts a local dance troupe to converge on the scene; they mesmerize the audience with their traditional movements and colorful costumes. One observer, an island visitor, gets up and joins the dance. A local man with a bead of sweat on his brow flashes her a bright smile and says, "Hey, you ever seen this before? This is the good stuff."

In This Chapter

the arts

PUERTO RICO HAS RICKY MARTIN, Jamaica has Bob Marley, and Aruba has . . . well, Aruba has a handful of stars who aren't quite as famous but are just as talented. Over the years, several local artists including composer Julio Renado Euson (who once won a competition against Ricky Martin), choreographer Wilma Kuiperi, sculptor Ciro Abath, and visual artist Elvis Lopez have gained international renown. Further, many Aruban musicians play more than one type of music (classical, jazz, soca, salsa, reggae, calypso, rap, pop), and many compose as well as perform.

The Union of Cultural Organizations is devoted to developing local arts while broadening its international appeal, according to director Pancho Geerman. UNOCA provides scholarships to help artists of all ages to participate in exhibitions, shows, and festivals. Although some internationally recognized stars have returned to Aruba to help promote the island's cultural growth, renowned conductor and pianist Eldin Juddan, president of the Association of Musicians Arubano, says the island needs to do more to promote local musicians. "There's a lot of talent, but professional guidance is needed to bring these talents and music to their potential. They [the professionals] can be instrumental in leading workshops, giving lectures, and organizing local performing- and visual-arts events. . . ."

The **CAS DI CULTURA** (Vondellaan 2, Oranjestad, tel. 297/8–21010), the island's cultural center, continuously hosts art exhibits, folkloric shows, dance performances, and concerts. Further, the island's many festivals showcase arts and culture.

Everybody on the Dance Floor

If you're lucky, during your stay in Aruba you might catch a performance by Claudius Philips. If so, be prepared to wriggle through a crowded dance floor. Philips—a singer, pianist, composer, and arranger—began performing at age 16. A year later he won his first competition during a song festival on St. Maarten. In the past 15 years, he has won the title of "Calypso King" 14 times and "Road March King" 10 times.

Claudius and Oreo, the 16-member band he founded in 1992, perform regularly on Aruba and have also played in Curaçao, Bonaire, St. Maarten, Suriname, Holland, and even the United States. Followers are no doubt drawn by the group's versatility; they play everything from calypso, salsa, and meringue to disco. Among the most popular songs are those about island happenings—both political and cultural—as well those that are just plain fun, such as "Saca e Boem Boem" ("Push Out Your Butt").

To find out what's going on, check out *Aruba Today*, the local newspaper, or *Calalou*, a Caribbean publication dedicated to the visual arts. You can also phone the national library, which has a bulletin board of events.

ART GALLERIES
GALERIA ETERNO. At this gallery you'll find local and international artists at work. Be sure to stop by for concerts by classical guitarists, dance performances, visual-arts shows, and plays. Emanstraat 92, Oranjestad, tel. 297/8–39607.

GALERIA HARMONIA. The island's largest gallery has changing art exhibits as well as a permanent collection of works by local and international artists. Zeppenfeldstraat 10, San Nicolas, tel. 297/8–42969.

GASPARITO RESTAURANT AND ART GALLERY. This exceptional dining spot features an ongoing exhibition of works by Aruban artists. Selected works are for sale. *Gasparito 3, Noord, tel. 297/8–67044.*

FESTIVALS

Annual Events

THE DANDE STROLL. New Year's Eve is a big deal in most places, but on Aruba, the fireworks that light up the sky at midnight are just the beginning. Celebrations continue throughout New Year's Day. Groups of musicians stroll from house to house, singing good-luck greetings for the new year. A prize is awarded to the group with the best song, which is sung by islanders during the next 12 months. Dande, by the way, comes from the Papiamento word "dandara," which means "to have a good time."

INTERNATIONAL DANCE FESTIVAL ARUBA. Each October, dance companies from the Caribbean, the United States, and Europe conduct and participate in workshops, lectures, demonstrations, and exhibitions.

INTERNATIONAL THEATRE FESTIVAL ARUBA. Every other October, theater groups from around the world perform 45- to 70-minute shows at the Cas Di Cultura.

JAZZ AND LATIN MUSIC FESTIVAL. For a few nights each June, you can hear authentic jazz and Latin music performed at the outdoor venue next to the Aruba Sonesta Resort at Seaport Village. There's a good deal of dancing in the aisles at this event. Tickets and hotel-package information are available from Aruba Tourism Authority offices.

HI-WINDS WORLD CHALLENGE. Windsurfers of all skill levels come from over 30 different countries during the first week of

Carnival

Aruba's biggest bash incorporates local traditions with those of Venezuela, Brazil, Holland, and North America. Here, Carnival consists of six weeks of jump-ups (traditional Caribbean street celebrations), competitions, parties, and colorful parades. The celebrations culminate with the Grand Parade held in Oranjestad on the Sunday before Ash Wednesday. It lasts for hours and turns the streets into one big stage. The two main events are the Grand Children's Parade, where kids dress in colorful costumes and decorate floats, and the Lightening Parade, consisting of miles of glittery floats and lavish costumes. Steel-pan and brass bands supply the music that inspires the crowds to dance. All events end on Shrove Tuesday: at midnight an effigy of King Momo (traditionally depicted as a fat man) is burned, indicating the end of joy and the beginning of Lenten penitence.

July to put the island's ideal wind and surf conditions to use in competition off the beaches at Fisherman's Huts at Hadicurari.

NATIONAL ANTHEM AND FLAG DAY. On this official holiday, held on March 18, you can stop by Plaza Betico Croes in Oranjestad for folkloric presentations and other traditional festivities.

ST. JOHN'S DAY. Dera Gai, the annual "burying of the rooster" festival, is celebrated on June 24, the Feast of St. John the Baptist. Festive songs, bright yellow and red costumes, and traditional dances mark this holiday dating from 1862. Today, the rooster—which symbolizes a successful harvest—has been replaced by a gourd.

Weekly Fetes

BON BINI FESTIVAL. This year-round folkloric event is held every Tuesday from 6:30 PM to 8:30 PM at the historic Fort Zoutman in Oranjestad. Stop by to check out the local arts and crafts, food, drink, music, and dance. The entrance fee is $3.

WATAPANA FOOD & ART FESTIVAL. Listen to live music, enjoy local art, and indulge in authentic Aruban foods and beverages at the festival grounds between the Hyatt Regency Aruba Beach Resort & Casino and the Allegro Aruba Beach Resort & Casino. Held from April to October, the event takes place every Wednesday from 6 PM to 8 PM. Admission is free.

A visitor from the United States became frustrated when he couldn't get in touch with his family—either via the Internet or his long-distance phone service—from his hotel. Another hotelier overheard the visitor complain about the problem to a beach buddy. The hotelier immediately offered to let the visitor use the facilities at his hotel, handing over a key to the private computer room. And, of course, the hotelier also invited the visitor to join him for coffee.

In This Chapter

where to stay

"CUIDA NOS TURISTA" **("TAKE CARE OF OUR TOURISTS")** is the island's motto, and Arubans are taught the finer points of hospitality as soon as they learn to read and write. With such cordial hosts, it's hard to go wrong no matter which accommodation you choose.

Most hotels are west of Oranjestad, along L. G. Smith and J. E. Irausquin boulevards. Many are self-contained complexes, with water-sports centers, health clubs, restaurants, shops, casinos, and car-rental and travel desks. Room service, laundry and dry-cleaning services, in-room safes, minibars or refrigerators, and baby-sitting are standard at all but the smallest properties. Most places don't include meals in their rates. Still, you can shop around for good dining options, as hotel restaurants and clubs are open to all island guests.

Many people prefer to stay in time-shares, returning year after year and making the island a kind of home away from home. Some time-share patrons say they like the spacious, homey accommodations and the opportunity to prepare their own meals. Note that hotel-type amenities such as shampoo, hair dryers, and housekeeping service may not be offered in time shares; if they are, they often cost extra. Also note that time-shares incur a daily occupancy tax of 18% (for Aruba Hotel and Tourism Association members) or 16.55% (for non-members) in lieu of the standard 6% hotel tax. Be sure to ask about taxes before booking.

At press time, plans were in the works to introduce a special program for frequent visitors to Aruba. This would include automatic check-in at the airport (sign in, get your key, and head

Associations That Accommodate

The **ARUBA HOTEL AND TOURISM ASSOCIATION** (tel. 297/8–22607) was established in 1965 to maintain high standards in the tourism industry. From its original seven hotels, the organization has grown into a powerhouse of more than 80 businesses, including restaurants, casinos, stores, tour operators, and airlines. The organization's $1 million annual budget, earmarked to promote Aruba as a travel destination, comes from the Aruba Tourism Authority and from private sector partners. It maintains a hot line (on the Aruba Tourism Web site at www.arubatourism.com) where you can express opinions and register complaints. The organization is also involved in island cleanup efforts as part of the Aruba Limpi Committee.

Another association, the **ARUBA APARTMENT RESORT AND SMALL HOTEL ASSOCIATION** (tel. 297/8–23289), represents smaller, less expensive hotels. Members are expected to meet certain standards of accommodations and service and still offer affordable rates (often as low as $65 per night).

right to your hotel room). Check with your travel agent to see if the plan has taken effect and whether you qualify. There are, however, a few perks already in place for repeat island visitors: return for 10 consecutive years, and a picture taken of you and a tourist board representative will be published in a local paper. Come for 20 years in a row and you'll be named a goodwill ambassador to the island.

Prices

Hotel rates are high; to save money, take advantage of airline and hotel packages, or visit during the summer when rates are discounted by as much as 40%. If you're traveling with kids, ask about discounts; children often stay for free in their parents' room, though there are age cutoffs.

CATEGORY	COST*
$$$$	over $325
$$$	$250–$325
$$	$175–$250
$	under $175

*All prices are for a standard double room during high season, excluding taxes and service charges.

$$$$ **ARUBA MARRIOTT RESORT & STELLARIS CASINO.** You'll hear the
★ sound of water everywhere at this high-rise hotel on Palm Beach, whether it's the beating of the surf below your balcony or the trickling of the waterfalls in the marble lobby and around the tropically landscaped pool. Spacious rooms have a distinctly Caribbean feeling. Most have ocean views, as well as walk-in closets, hair dryers, and irons. The path to the ocean from the garden-view rooms is longer than that from elsewhere in the complex, but the in-room hot tubs more than compensate for this. Tuscany offers superlative Italian cuisine, and Simply Fish serves up dishes fresh from the sea. Express checkout is available. L. G. Smith Blvd. 101, Palm Beach, tel. 297/8–69000 or 800/223–6388, fax 297/8–60649, www.marriott.com. 413 rooms, 20 suites. 4 restaurants, 4 bars, café, in-room data ports, in-room safes, minibars, cable TV with movies, in-room VCRs, 2 tennis courts, pool, aerobics, hair salon, health club, massage, saunas, spa, beach, dive shop, windsurfing, boating, jet skiing, volleyball, casino, shops, concierge, Internet, meeting rooms, car rental. AE, D, DC, MC, V. EP, FAP, MAP.

$$$$ **COSTA LINDA BEACH RESORT.** The name of this hotel, Spanish for "beautiful coast," speaks for itself. This paradise on earth is on a 183-m (600-ft) stretch of pristine Eagle Beach. An inviting blue pool sits in the center of the manicured grounds. A blend of Dutch, Spanish, and Portuguese influences is evident in the architecture. Pamper yourself with numerous amenities in the bright, spacious two-bedroom suites, including Roman tubs, hair dryers, and balconies overlooking the crystalline sea. Larger units also have outdoor hot tubs and barbecue grills. There are lighted tennis courts on the premises, and scuba diving, snorkeling,

lodging

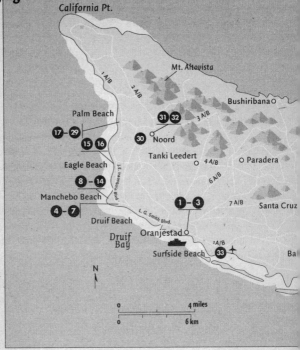

Allegro Aruba
Resort &
Casino, 20

Amsterdam Manor
Beach Resort, 16

Aruba Beach
Club, 12

Aruba Grand
Beach Resort &
Casino, 22

Aruba Marriott
Resort & Stellaris
Casino, 18

Aruba Millennium
Resort, 25

Aruba Phoenix
Beach Resort, 28

Aruba Sonesta
Resort, 1

Boardwalk
Vacation
Retreat, 29

Brickell Bay Beach
Club, 27

Bucuti Beach
Resort, 10

Bushiri Beach
Resort, 9

La Cabana All
Suite Beach
Resort &
Casino, 15

Caribbean Palm
Village, 31

Casa Del Mar
Beach Resort, 3

Coconut Inn, 32

Costa Linda Beach
Resort, 13

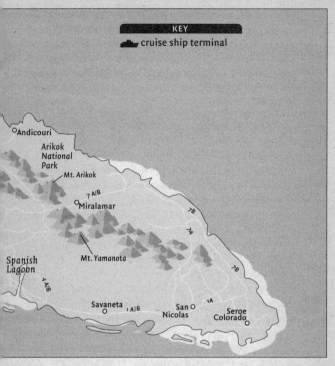

KEY

cruise ship terminal

Andicouri

Arikok National Park

Mt. Arikok

7 A|B

Miralamar

7B

7A

Mt. Yamanota

Spanish Lagoon

4 A|B

7B

Savaneta

1 A|B

San Nicolas

1A

Seroe Colorado

Divi Aruba Beach Resort Mega All Inclusive, 5

Divi Village, 6

Dutch Village, 7

Holiday Inn Sunspree Aruba Beach Resort & Casino, 23

Hyatt Regency Aruba Beach Resort & Casino, 19

Manchebo Beach Resort, 11

Marriott Aruba Ocean Club, 17

Mill Resort & Suites, 30

Paradise Beach Villas, 8

Playa Linda Beach Resort, 26

La Quinta Beach Resort, 14

Radisson Aruba Resort & Casino, 24

Talk of the Town Resort, 2

Tamarijn Aruba All Inclusive Beach Resort, 4

Vistalmar, 33

Wyndham Aruba Beach Resort & Casino, 21

and boating opportunities nearby. In the evening, head to the resort's nightclub or walk to the Alhambra Casino. J. E. Irausquin Blvd. 59, Eagle Beach, tel. 297/8–38000, fax 297/8–36040, www. costalinda-aruba.com. 155 suites. 2 restaurants, 2 bars, kitchenettes, refrigerators, cable TV, 2 tennis courts, pool, wading pool, health club, shops, baby-sitting, children's programs, dry cleaning, laundry facilities, Internet. AE, DC, MC, V. BP, CP, EP, MAP.

$$$$ ★ HYATT REGENCY ARUBA BEACH RESORT & CASINO. A favorite among honeymooners, this resort looks like a Spanish palace, with art deco–style flourishes and a multilevel pool with waterfalls, a two-story water slide, and a lagoon stocked with tropical fish and black swans. Rooms have slim balconies, but lots of extras; those on the Regency Club floor have such amenities as complimentary breakfast and concierge service. Relax on the beach, play tennis, or head out for a horseback ride before an afternoon hydrotherapy treatment and a stop at the juice bar. For a full meal choose from excellent restaurants, including Ruinas del Mar, where you'll find Continental fare, and Japengo, serving up seafood with an Asian flair. Parents appreciate the imaginative Camp Hyatt, which incorporates Aruban storytelling, cooking, and arts and crafts for kids ages 3–12. J. E. Irausquin Blvd. 85, Palm Beach, tel. 297/8–61234 or 800/554–9288, fax 297/8–61682, www.hyatt.com. 342 rooms, 18 suites. 5 restaurants, 5 bars, snack bar, room service, fans, in-room safes, minibars, cable TV with movies, 2 tennis courts, pool, salon, health club, 2 outdoor hot tubs, massage, sauna, spa, steam room, beach, dive shop, dock, snorkeling, windsurfing, boating, jet skiing, waterskiing, basketball, horseback riding, volleyball, casino, shops, baby-sitting, children's programs, playground, concierge, business services, Internet, car rental, travel services, some pets allowed. AE, D, DC, MC, V. EP, MAP.

$$$$ ★ MARRIOTT ARUBA OCEAN CLUB. First-rate amenities and lavishly decorated villas have made this time share the talk of the island. Each one- and two-bedroom unit includes a kitchen and a balcony with a spectacular ocean view. The S-shape pool has a swim-up bar and waterfalls; there are four hot tubs built into the rocks above.

You can access facilities at the adjacent Aruba Marriott Resort & Stellaris Casino, including the spa, the fitness center, and the casino. *L. G. Smith Blvd. 101, Palm Beach, tel. 297/8–62641, fax 297/8–68000, www.marriott.com. 218 units. Restaurant, grocery, kitchenettes, refrigerators, microwaves, cable TV with movies, pool, spa, beach, dive shop, snorkeling, windsurfing, boating, jet skiing, shops, Internet, meeting rooms. AE, D, DC, MC, V. BP, EP.*

$$$$ **RADISSON ARUBA RESORT & CASINO.** Aruba's newest and largest
★ hotel reopened at the start of this century with a promise to pamper its guests. Exotic birds greet you in the expansive lobby. Colonial Caribbean–style guest rooms (each with a view of the ocean or the garden) have mahogany four-poster beds and such singular accents as hand-beaded lamp shades. The designers thought of everything: blue accent lighting, wood furniture on the balconies, and plantation shutters. In-room perks include minibars (careful, they're touch-sensored), coffeemakers, and hair dryers. Unwind in the fitness center and spa, then enjoy a meal at one of the hotel's excellent restaurants. Try Gilligan's at the beach for simple fare, or the Sunset Grille for more elaborate dishes. *J. E. Irausquin Boulevard 81, Palm Beach, tel. 297/8–66555, fax 297/8–63260, www.radisson.com. 358 rooms, 32 suites. 4 restaurants, 3 bars, room service, in-room safes, minibars, cable TV with movies, golf privileges, 2 tennis courts, 2 pools, health club, spa, beach, dive shop, snorkeling, boating, jet skiing, video game rooms, baby-sitting, children's programs, dry cleaning, laundry service, business services, convention center, Internet, meeting rooms. AE, D, DC, MC, V. BP, FAP, MAP.*

$$$$ **TAMARIJN ARUBA ALL INCLUSIVE BEACH RESORT.** Low-rise buildings stretch along the shore at this all-inclusive resort catering to couples and families. The spacious oceanfront rooms, filled with light-wood furnishings, have private balconies. The rate covers food, beverages, entertainment, an array of activities, and even tickets to the weekly Bon Bini Festival. A bar at one end of the property serves food and drinks as a convenience for guests more removed from the main restaurants. Utilize the free shuttle

that runs to the Alhambra Casino until 3 AM. J. E. Irausquin Blvd. 41, Punta Brabo, tel. 297/8–24150 or 800/554–2008, fax 297/8–31940, www.tamarijnaruba.com. 236 rooms. 3 restaurants, 2 bars, snack bar, fans, cable TV, 2 tennis courts, 2 pools, health club, beach, snorkeling, windsurfing, boating, waterskiing, fishing, bicycles, Ping-Pong, shuffleboard, volleyball, shops, Internet, meeting rooms, car rental. AE, D, DC, MC, V. All-inclusive.

$$$$ WYNDHAM ARUBA BEACH RESORT & CASINO. From exciting windsurfing to sizzling nightlife, the Wyndham seems to have something for everyone. Grand public areas accommodate big groups from North and South America, which make up a good portion of the clientele. Rooms, which are oddly configured, have mustard-color stucco walls and handsome dark-wood furniture. All have ocean-view balconies and amenities like coffeemakers, refrigerators, and hair dryers. A day at the pool means more than swimming and sunning; a "pool concierge" makes the rounds, loaning out books, magazines, and CD players; pool attendants spritz you with Evian, offer chilled towels, and serve frozen drinks. If you still don't feel pampered, head to the health club for a massage, facial, or sauna. From there, you're only steps from the beach to dig your toes into the fine white sand. J. E. Irausquin Blvd. 77, Palm Beach, tel. 297/8–64466 or 800/996–3426, fax 297/8–68217, www.wyndham.com. 481 rooms, 81 suites. 5 restaurants, 6 bars, in-room safes, cable TV, tennis court, pool, wading pool, 2 outdoor hot tubs, hair salon, health club, massage, sauna, steam room, beach, dive shop, snorkeling, windsurfing, boating, jet skiing, parasailing, waterskiing, Ping-Pong, shuffleboard, volleyball, casino, video game room, shops, concierge, convention center, Internet. AE, D, DC, MC, V. All-inclusive, CP, EP, FAP, MAP.

$$$ LA CABANA ALL SUITE BEACH RESORT & CASINO. Across the road from Eagle Beach you'll find this self-contained resort. The original four-story building facing the surf surrounds two pools, a bar, and a restaurant. About a third of the studios and one-bedroom suites have ocean views. All have kitchenettes, balconies, and even hot tubs. Pricier villas are away from the main building near a parking lot. The hotel's "home food shopping program" means someone else does the legwork during your stay. You can order groceries on line up to two days prior to your vacation and have them delivered when you arrive. J. E. Irausquin Blvd. 250, Eagle Beach, tel. 297/8–79000; 212/251–1710 in NY; 800/835–7193; fax 297/8–70834, www.lacabana.com. 803 suites. 3 restaurants, 5 bars, grocery, ice cream parlor, in-room safes, kitchenettes, microwaves, cable TV, 5 tennis courts, 3 pools, aerobics, health club, 3 outdoor hot tubs, massage, sauna, spa, dive shop, basketball, racquetball, shuffleboard, squash, volleyball, video game room, shops, playground, Internet, meeting rooms. AE, DC, MC, V. All-inclusive, EP, FAP, MAP.

$$$ PLAYA LINDA BEACH RESORT. It's hard to separate fantasy from reality at this luscious pyramid-shaped resort. Set right on a sandy white beach, luxurious studios and one- and two-bedroom suites are spacious and lavishly appointed. Frolic on the beach, dip in the free-form pool or one of the hot tubs, play a few games of tennis, or shop in the arcade. After dining at the Linda Vista International restaurant or preparing a meal in your fully equipped kitchen, shun the radio and satellite TV in favor of the sea view from the large terrace. Other evening entertainment options include the free weekly cocktail party. Come morning, grab a quick bite at on-site Dushi Bagels. J. E. Irausquin Blvd. 87, Palm Beach, tel. 297/8–61000, fax 297/8–65210, www.playalinda.com. 200 units. Restaurant, 2 bars, in-room safes, kitchenettes, refrigerators, cable TV, putting green, 3 tennis courts, pool, health club, hot tub, beach, dive shop, windsurfing, boating, fishing, shops, video game room, baby-sitting, laundry facilities, Internet, meeting rooms. AE, D, DC, MC, V. CP.

$$–$$$ ARUBA GRAND BEACH RESORT & CASINO. Regulars return again and again to this beachfront resort for its relaxed atmosphere. The yellow and white building, with its distinctive jade green roof, is accompanied by 55 thatch-roof beach huts. Large rooms and suites have such amenities as generous walk-in closets and balconies that overlook either the ocean, the pool, or the garden. The Seawatch restaurant offers international cuisine for breakfast, lunch, and dinner; the more casual Whale's Rib entices seafood lovers with its fresh fish. Ask about packages; discounts are available for children under 12. J. E. Irausquin Blvd. 79, Palm Beach, tel. 297/8–63900 or 800/345–2782, fax 297/8–61941, www. arubagrand.com. 130 rooms, 41 suites. 2 restaurants, 3 bars, ice cream parlor, snack bar, room service, in-room safes, refrigerators, cable TV, 2 tennis courts, pool, wading pool, beach, dive shop, snorkeling, windsurfing, boating, waterskiing, volleyball, casino, shops, baby-sitting, dry cleaning, laundry service, concierge, Internet, meeting rooms. AE, D, DC, MC, V. All-inclusive, EP, MAP.

$$–$$$ **ARUBA SONESTA RESORT.** For those who enjoy being in the thick
★ of things, this lively resort is surrounded by shops, restaurants, and casinos. It's a top choice for singles, yet also has plenty of activities for families. Seniors appreciate the discounted room rates. The newer building—whose roomy suites have kitchenettes—is near a private beach. The original high-rise has compact but attractive rooms; choose the quieter garden-view rooms. In the lobby, connected to the Seaport Mall, you can board a skiff for a day trip to the resort's 40-acre private island. The gourmet restaurant, L'Escale, is one of Aruba's best. L. G. Smith Blvd. 9, Oranjestad, tel. 297/8–36000 or 800/766–3782, fax 297/8–25317, www.arubasonesta.com. 300 rooms, 265 suites. 4 restaurants, 5 bars, room service, kitchenettes, minibars, some microwaves, cable TV with movies, golf privileges, tennis court, 3 pools, gym, massage, spa, beach, dive shop, snorkeling, marina, fishing, volleyball, 2 casinos, nightclub, video game room, shops, children's programs, playground, laundry facilities, concierge, convention center, Internet, meeting rooms; no-smoking rooms. AE, D, DC, MC, V. EP, FAP, MAP.

$$–$$$ **BUCUTI BEACH RESORT.** Owner Ewald Biemans was named the
★ island's hotelier of the year for the second year in a row for his refreshingly peaceful European-style resort. Popular with honeymooners (who receive champagne and romantic goodies upon arrival), the hacienda-style buildings house sunny rooms with handsome cherrywood furnishings, sparkling tile floors,

and ocean-view terraces. Extras include coffeemakers, microwaves, and hair dryers. The grounds are lushly landscaped, and the intimate resort has an enviable location on the widest, most secluded section of Eagle Beach. Work out in the open-air exercise pavilion and stay connected using the hotel's rare 24-hour access to the Internet. The resort also won an award in 2001 for being environmentally conscientious. *L. G. Smith Blvd. 55-B, Eagle Beach, tel. 297/8–31100, fax 297/8–25272, www.bucuti.com. 58 rooms, 5 suites. Restaurant, bar, grocery, fans, in-room safes, minibars, microwaves, refrigerators, cable TV, pool, beach, bicycles, shop, laundry facilities, business services, Internet, travel services. AE, D, DC, MC, V. CP, MAP.*

$$–$$$ DIVI ARUBA BEACH RESORT MEGA ALL INCLUSIVE. At this Mediterranean-style resort, you have your choice of standard rooms, beachfront lanais, or casitas that overlook courtyards and are often only steps from the beach. The white-tile floors and mint and jade color schemes are soothing. Make your own daiquiri at the poolside Pelican Bar, where you can also enjoy pizza hot from the oven. In addition to the many on-site facilities, you can also use those at the adjacent Tamarijn Aruba. Despite the "mega all-inclusive" label, getting your laundry done, having your hair cut, or hiring a baby-sitter costs extra. *L. G. Smith Blvd. 93, Manchebo Beach, tel. 297/8–23300 or 800/554–2008, fax 297/8–31940, www.diviaruba.com. 203 rooms. 5 restaurants, 3 bars, fans, refrigerators, cable TV, tennis court, 2 pools, gym, hair salon, outdoor hot tub, beach, dive shop, snorkeling, windsurfing, boating, waterskiing, bicycles, shuffleboard, volleyball, shops, baby-sitting, laundry service, Internet. AE, D, DC, MC, V. All-inclusive.*

$$–$$$ HOLIDAY INN SUNSPREE ARUBA BEACH RESORT & CASINO. Three seven-story buildings filled with spacious rooms are set apart from each other along a sugary, palm-dotted shore. The pool's cascades and sundeck draw as large a crowd as the wide beach, where you're invited to the Monday evening cocktail party. Enjoy live entertainment as you try your luck at the casino, or savor a beachfront meal at the Sea Breeze Grill. Get massaged and wrapped at the new Intermezzo Spa. At press time, plans were in the works to expand the fitness center—one of the final stages of a multi-million dollar renovation that began at the turn of the millennium. The resort has a free club for kids ages 5 to 12. *J. E. Irausquin Blvd. 230, Palm Beach, tel. 297/8–60236 or 800/934–6750 (direct to hotel), fax 297/8–60323, www.holidayinn-aruba.com. 600 rooms, 15 suites. 3 restaurants, 3 bars, refrigerators, cable TV with movies, 4 tennis courts, 2 pools, gym, massage, beach, dive shop, dock, snorkeling, windsurfing, boating, waterskiing, basketball, Ping-Pong, volleyball, casino, video game room, shops, children's programs, concierge, Internet, meeting rooms. AE, DC, MC, V. All-inclusive, EP, FAP, MAP.*

$$–$$$ PARADISE BEACH VILLAS. Decorated in shades of peach, these air-conditioned suites (some accessible to people with disabilities) have spacious bedrooms, fully equipped kitchens, hot tubs, and large balconies with pool or ocean views. This low-rise resort attracts many perennial visitors—the sophisticated set that returns here year after year is generally over 30. Splash around at one of the two large pools or mellow out with a dip in an outdoor whirlpool. Relieve stress with a strawberry daiquiri from the poolside bar or head to the rooftop deck for a margarita at the Star Gazer bar. For more action, try the water sports—from banana boat rides to jet-skiing jaunts—at the nearby beach. On-site conveniences include a drugstore and a small grocery. *L. G. Smith Blvd., Eagle Beach, tel. 297/8–74000, fax 297/8–70071, paradisebeachvillas.com. 80 units. 2 restaurants, 2 bars, grocery, kitchenettes, microwaves, refrigerators, 2 pools, gym, 2 hot tubs, beach, shops, Internet, meeting room. AE, D, MC, V. EP.*

$$ ALLEGRO ARUBA RESORT & CASINO. Activity surrounds the cloverleaf-shape pool (with its waterfall and whirlpool tubs) at the heart of this resort. A popular place with tour groups, it has a buzzing atmosphere where you can enjoy everything from beer-drinking contests to bikini shows. The tropical-themed rooms have white-tile bathrooms that are snug and balconies that are narrow step-outs, but improvements include better air-conditioning. The Kids' Club, open from 9 to 5 daily, keeps children ages 4 to 12 busy with a wide range of activities. *J. E. Irausquin Blvd. 83, Palm Beach, tel. 297/8–64500 or 800/447–7462, fax 297/8–63191, www.allegroresorts.com. 403 rooms, 14 suites. 3 restaurants, 3 bars, in-room safes, cable TV with movies, 2 tennis courts, pool, gym, 2 outdoor hot tubs, beach, snorkeling, boating, waterskiing, basketball, Ping-Pong, volleyball, casino, dance club, shops, children's programs, Internet, meeting rooms. AE, D, DC, MC, V. All-inclusive.*

$$ AMSTERDAM MANOR BEACH RESORT. This mustard yellow hotel—all gables and turrets—looks like part of a Dutch colonial village. It's a cozy enclave surrounding a pool with a waterfall. Glorious Eagle Beach is just across the street. Rooms are furnished in either Dutch modern or provincial style and range from small studios—some with private balconies—to two-bedroom suites with peaked ceilings, full kitchens, and whirlpool tubs. Children under 12 stay free with their parents. Free diving lessons are available, and the hotel can arrange a variety of other activities. *J. E. Irausquin Blvd. 252, Eagle Beach, tel. 297/8–71492 or 800/932–6509, fax 297/8–71463, www.amsterdammanor.com. 70 units. Restaurant, bar, fans, in-room safes, kitchenettes, microwaves, cable TV with movies, pool, wading pool, snorkeling, playground, laundry facilities, Internet, car rental, some pets allowed. AE, DC, MC, V. CP, EP, MAP.*

$$ ARUBA BEACH CLUB. Colonial charm and Dutch hospitality create an ambience that keeps people coming back. All studios and one-bedroom units in this time-share property have bamboo furniture, satellite TVs, and balconies, sometimes with ocean views. There's plenty to do here, including yoga and language courses in Papiamento. The front desk can arrange for water sports and other activities. Kids enjoy the playground as well as their own pool. A shopping arcade is filled with boutiques, a frozen yogurt shop, and a cybercafé. If all this isn't enough, you can use the facilities at the adjoining Casa del Mar Beach Resort. J. E. Irausquin Blvd. 53, Manchebo Beach, tel. 297/8–23000, fax 297/8–26557, www.arubabeachclub.com. 89 rooms, 42 suites. Restaurant, bar, café, cable TV, Internet, video game room, meeting rooms, grocery, in-room safes, kitchenettes, 2 tennis courts, pool, wading pool, hair salon, health club, shops, baby-sitting, children's programs, playground, laundry service, car rental, travel services. AE, D, DC, MC, V. EP.

$$ ARUBA PHOENIX BEACH RESORT. A breathtaking location and a lively atmosphere make the Aruba Phoenix justifiably popular. In many of the studio and one- or two-bedroom units you'll find balconies with ocean views. Tropical color schemes, wood furnishings, and lots of plants make you feel at home. Coffeemakers, microwaves, and hair dryers are among the thoughtful touches. Some rooms are wheelchair accessible. In the evenings, enjoy live entertainment or try your luck at the nearby Alhambra Casino. J. E. Irausquin Blvd. 75, Palm Beach, tel. 297/8–66066, fax 297/8–61165, www.diviphoenix.com. 101 units. Restaurant, 2 bars, grocery, snack bar, fans, in-room safes, kitchenettes, refrigerators, cable TV, in-room VCRs, pool, health club, hot tub, beach, snorkeling, boating, volleyball, shop, children's programs, Internet, meeting rooms, travel services. AE, D, DC, MC, V. EP.

$$ BOARDWALK VACATION RETREAT. The owners describe this small hotel as offering "far-from-it-all tranquillity with close-to-it-all convenience." A stay here puts you only a few yards from the beach and water sports and within walking distance of casinos. The suites are in casitas enveloped by gardens where hummingbirds and butterflies dart among the exotic palm trees. The rooms have comfortable rattan furnishings, large living rooms and kitchens, and patios with barbecue grills and hammocks. Housekeeping is provided every other day, and laundry service is available. Bakval 20, Palm Beach, tel. 297/8–66654, fax 297/8–61836, www.theboardwalk-aruba.com. 13 units. Grocery, kitchenettes, microwaves, refrigerators, cable TV, in-room VCRs, pool, wading pool, hot tub, baby-sitting. AE, MC, V. EP.

$$ BUSHIRI BEACH RESORT. A small, sandy cove that's a 20-minute walk from Oranjestad is the setting for this low-rise all-inclusive resort. There's plenty to do here, such as Papiamento language courses, arts-and-crafts classes, tennis clinics, scuba diving lessons, and nightly entertainment. One restaurant serves Italian fare; a more casual restaurant offers a breakfast buffet and lunch. Food, beverages, activities, airport transfers, and gratuities are included in the rate. *L. G. Smith Blvd. 35, Punta Brabo, tel. 297/8–25216, fax 297/8–26789, www.bushiri.com. 155 rooms. 2 restaurants, bar, fans, cable TV, 2 tennis courts, pool, wading pool, health club, 3 hot tubs, beach, dive shop, snorkeling, boating, 2 shops, video game room, baby-sitting, children's programs, laundry service, car rental, travel services. AE, D, DC, MC, V. All-inclusive.*

$$ CARIBBEAN PALM VILLAGE. Lush gardens lend an air of tranquillity to this tile-roofed resort not far from Palm Beach. The one- or two-bedroom suites have fully equipped kitchens and private balconies. The pool bar serves up breakfast and lunch; after enjoying the light fare you can serve up a few aces on the tennis court. Enjoy a romantic rendezvous at Valentino's Italian restaurant, or make your own meal in the barbecue area. The hotel, a short walk from casinos, nightclubs, and water sports, generally attracts professionals over 30. A convenience store, shopping center, and doctor's office are also just steps away. Although Eagle Beach is only a 10-minute walk from the resort, there is daily transportation to and from this sandy stretch of shoreline; buses depart at 9:25 AM and 2:25 PM and return at 12:30 PM and 4 PM. *Palm Beach Rd., Noord 43E, Noord, tel. 297/8–62700, fax 297/8–62380. 170 suites. Restaurant, bar, fans, kitchenettes, microwaves, refrigerators, cable TV, tennis court, 2 pools, hot tub, baby-sitting, car rental. AE, DC, MC, V. EP.*

$$ CASA DEL MAR BEACH RESORT. This beachside resort offers two parts recreation, one part rest and relaxation. Deluxe accommodations are quite comfortable, with amenities like balconies and fully equipped kitchens. Play tennis on one of four lighted courts, work out in the exercise room, arrange water

Rest Easy

Even the softest of sheets can feel scratchy against sun-burnt skin. Before bed, try a local product made with the aloe vera plant—an Aruban treasure that's been cultivated here since the 1840s. The gel from inside the plant's fibrous, water-retaining leaves is the key skin-moisturizing ingredient in Burn Balm, made by **ARUBA ALOE BALM** (tel. 800/95–27822, www.arubaaloe.com). Besides this great after-sun soother, the company also puts aloe in everything from lipstick to soap to hair spray.

If a pre-bed application of an aloe product doesn't soothe your sun-kissed skin, perhaps a local sleeplessness remedy will. The rest of the world may resort to counting sheep, but Aruban insomniacs turn to basil. Babies who can't settle in are given an herbal tea made from the tops of the white basil plant, which grows everywhere on the island. If your valerian root doesn't do the trick, a more potent version of this tea just might.

sports at the activities desk, or kick back with a book from the library. Relax at the daily happy hour and dine on fine Italian cuisine at the waterfront La Gondola restaurant. Kids ages 4–10 will enjoy the special programs offered weekdays from 10 to noon; on Tuesday all the wee ones are invited to the 6 PM pizza party. L. G. Smith Boulevard 51–53, Manchebo Beach, tel. 297/8–23000 or 297/8–27000, fax 297/8–38191, www.casadelmar-aruba.com. 147 suites. Restaurant, bar, grocery, in-room safes, kitchenettes, refrigerators, cable TV with movies, 4 tennis courts, 2 pools, wading pool, hair salon, hot tub, beach, library, video game room, shops, children's programs, laundry facilities, Internet, car rental, travel services. AE, D, DC, MC, V. EP.

$$ **DIVI VILLAGE.** A tropical feel pervades this self-contained time-share resort across the street from the beach. Accommodations here run the gamut from efficiencies to penthouses. Satellite TV,

full kitchens, and private balconies or patios are among the amenities. Enjoy tennis and water sports, then head off to the shops, restaurants, and clubs at the adjacent Divi Aruba, Dutch Village, and Tamarijn Aruba resorts. The Alhambra Casino is nearby. *J. E. Irausquin Blvd. 47, Punta Brabo, tel. 297/8–35000 or 800/367–3484, fax 297/8–20501, www.diviresorts.com. 153 units. Restaurant, bar, kitchenettes, microwaves, refrigerators, cable TV, tennis court. AE, DC, MC, V. EP.*

$$ LA QUINTA BEACH RESORT. A relaxed atmosphere makes this time-share resort so appealing. One-, two-, and three-bedroom apartments have living-dining areas and kitchenettes. Daily housekeeping is a real perk. All suites have balconies with either garden or ocean views. The resort is adjacent to the Alhambra Casino and across the street from the beach. Enjoy a hearty meal at Fiorentio, the resort's new restaurant. *L. G. Smith Blvd. 228, Eagle Beach, tel. 297/8–75010, fax 297/8–76263, www.webnova. com/laquinta. 54 units. Restaurant, bar, kitchenettes, refrigerators, microwaves, cable TV, 2 pools, outdoor hot tub, nightclub, baby-sitting, laundry service, Internet, car rental. AE, MC, V. EP.*

$$ MANCHEBO BEACH RESORT. Set amid 100 acres of gardens, this resort feels away from it all. But it's just five minutes from town and right across from the Alhambra complex of shops, restaurants, and a casino. The international clientele appreciates a bargain (children under 12 stay free). Rooms are decorated with blond-wood furnishings and bright floral fabrics and are equipped with amenities such as coffeemakers. Popular with diners from all over the island, the French Steakhouse is renowned for its *churrasco* (Argentine mixed grill). The chapel, on one of the prettiest stretches of Eagle Beach, is a charming spot for weddings. *J. E. Irausquin Blvd. 55, Eagle Beach, tel. 297/8–23444 or 800/528–1234, fax 297/8–33667 or 297/8–32446, aruba-manchebo.com. 71 rooms. 2 restaurants, 2 bars, snack bar, fans, in-room safes, refrigerators, cable TV, pool, beach, dive shop, snorkeling, shops, Internet, car rental. AE, D, DC, MC, V. EP, MAP.*

$$ MILL RESORT & SUITES. With clean geometric lines, the architecture of this small resort is striking. The award-winning resort's whitewashed, red-roof buildings surround its open-air common areas. After a 2001 renovation, rooms are brighter and more attractive. Junior suites have sitting areas and kitchenettes. Smaller studios have full kitchens, tiny baths, and no balconies. The beach is only a five-minute walk away; a morning coffee hour and a weekly scuba lesson are among the on-site amenities. At the Garden Café a special menu offers three courses at affordable prices. Board Fido or Fluffy overnight at the nearby vet. *J. E. Irausquin Blvd. 330, Oranjestad, tel. 297/8–67700, fax 297/8–67271, www.millresort.com. 64 studios, 128 suites. Restaurant, bar, grill, grocery, in-room safes, kitchenettes, microwaves, cable TV, 2 tennis courts, 2 pools, wading pool, gym, hair salon, massage, saunas, shops, laundry facilities, Internet, car rental, travel services, some pets allowed. AE, D, DC, MC, V. EP.*

$–$$ DUTCH VILLAGE. Enjoy Old World ambience while basking in New World comforts at this oceanfront time-share complex set around a pair of free-form freshwater pools. Many handcrafted accents adorn the Spanish-style rooms, which have kitchens, hot tubs, and private patios. You can participate in various outdoor activities and dine in one of several restaurants at the adjoining Divi Aruba, Divi Village, and Tamarijn Aruba resorts. Steps away, the Alhambra Casino offers opportunities for shopping and gambling. *J. E. Irausquin Blvd. 47, Punta Brabo, tel. 297/8–35000 or 800/376–3484, fax 297/8–20501, www.diviresorts.com. 97 units. Kitchenettes, microwaves, refrigerators, cable TV, 2 pools, hot tubs, beach, Internet, some pets allowed. AE, D, DC, MC, V. EP.*

$ ARUBA MILLENNIUM RESORT. A two-minute walk from Palm Beach, this relaxed resort has studio and one-bedroom apartments that are sleekly furnished and decorated in subdued shades of blue and yellow. In-room amenities include well-equipped kitchens, separate dining rooms, and balconies. Dip into one of four whirlpools right outside your door, read on the sundeck, or

An Aruban Lullaby

This quirky little lullaby has been passed down from generation to generation on Aruba. Once they hear it, children generally go right to sleep—out of fear.

PAPIAMENTO:

Riba Cero di Biento
Ting Un Baca Malucu,
Muchanan Cu Ta Yora
Baca Ta Bin Come Nan.

ENGLISH:

On the windy mountain
There is a cranky cow,
And when children cry
The cow comes and eats them.

chat with other guests at the poolside bar. Glitzy casinos and fine restaurants are within walking distance. For longer stays, inquire about weekly and monthly rates. *Palm Beach Rd. 33, Palm Beach, tel. 297/8–61120, fax 297/8–62506, www.arubamillenniumresort.com. 32 units. Bar, fans, kitchenettes, microwaves, refrigerators, cable TV, pool, 4 outdoor hot tubs, mini-market; no-smoking rooms. AE, MC, V. EP.*

$ **BRICKELL BAY BEACH CLUB.** Formerly the Stauffer Hotel, this simple and comfortable place is well-situated across the street from the high-rises of Palm Beach. It's a 10-minute walk from the most popular shopping areas. There's no grand ocean view, but renovations brightened the rooms—they're painted sunny yellow—and added the sparkling pool and the Salt and Pepper restaurant. There's a bus stop nearby, but the convenient golf carts that run to and from the beach can't be beat. The owner also runs the Excelsior Casino, so you'll get a five dollar bill at check-in to start you out at the tables. J. E. Irausquin Blvd. 370, Palm Beach, tel. 297/8–60900, fax 297/8–64957, brickellbayaruba.com. 101 rooms. Restaurant, grocery, cable TV, pool, video game room, Internet, meeting rooms, some pets allowed. AE, D, DC, MC, V.

$ **COCONUT INN.** Set amid soaring palms, this budget motel in the countryside offers studios or one-bedroom suites with amenities such as TVs, direct-dial phones, and full kitchens. The mahogany headboards seem right at home amid the turquoise-tinged fabrics. Although it's not on the beach, the motel has a pool and a sundeck lined with cabanas; the island's finest sandy stretches and the major casinos are only a few minutes away. It's a short walk to the public bus stop and conveniences such as a supermarket, a pharmacy, banks, and restaurants. Noord 31, Noord, tel. 297/8–66288, fax 297/8–65433, www.coconutinn.com. 40 units. Restaurant, bar, kitchenettes, microwaves, refrigerators, cable TV, pool, laundry service. MC, V. BP.

$ **TALK OF THE TOWN RESORT.** A palm-lined courtyard, complete with a pool, a hot tub, and an open-air bar and restaurant, adorns this cozy resort attracting a young crowd. All of the brightly decorated rooms have amenities such as kitchenettes; some are accessible to people with disabilities. A stay here gets you free access to the private Havana Beach Club across the street, which has a dive shop and a bar and grill. Stop by the nightly happy hour. L. G. Smith Blvd. 2, Oranjestad, tel. 297/8–23380, fax 297/8–32446. 63 rooms. Restaurant, bar, in-room safes, cable TV, microwaves, kitchenettes, refrigerators, 2 pools, hot tub, laundry service, meeting rooms. AE, MC, V. BP, MAP.

$ **VISTALMAR.** When Alby and Katy Yarzagary met at a Christmas party more than 20 years ago, they clicked. After they wed, they converted this property across the street from the fishing pier into a homey inn. Their hospitality infuses every part of the place. Simply furnished one-bedroom apartments each have a full kitchen, a living-dining room, and a sunny porch. The Yarzagarys provide snorkel gear and stock the refrigerator with breakfast fixings. There's no beach, but the sea is just across the street. One drawback is the distance from town, but you can ride the bus that departs from the hotel five times daily or rent a car. *Bucutiweg 28, south of Oranjestad, tel. 297/8–28579, fax 297/8–22200. 8 rooms. Kitchenettes, microwaves, cable TV with movies, laundry facilities, car rental. No credit cards. CP.*

practical information

Addresses

"Informal" might best describe Aruban addresses. Sometimes the street designation is in English (as in J. E. Irausquin Blvd.), other times in Dutch (as in Wilhelminastraat); sometimes it's not specified whether something is a boulevard or a *straat* (street) at all. Street numbers follow street names, and postal codes aren't used at all. In rural areas, you might have to ask a local for directions—and be prepared for such instructions as "Take a right at the market, then a left where you see the big divi-divi tree."

Air Travel

Flights arrive daily on Aruba from New York area airports and Miami International Airport, with easy connections from most American cities. Flights are also offered (sometimes via Curaçao) from other American cities, including Atlanta, Baltimore, Houston, Philadelphia, and Tampa. Some airlines fly to the island via San Juan, Puerto Rico.

BOOKING YOUR FLIGHT

When you book **look for nonstop flights** and **remember that "direct" flights stop at least once.** Try to avoid connecting flights, which require a change of plane. Two airlines may operate a connecting flight jointly, so ask if your airline operates every segment of the trip; you may find that the carrier you prefer flies you only part of the way. To find more booking tips and to check prices and make on-line flight reservations, log on to www.fodors.com.

CARRIERS

Air ALM flies daily from Miami via Curaçao, twice a week nonstop from Atlanta, and twice a week from San Juan, Puerto Rico, through Curaçao. The airline also has connecting flights to Caracas, Bonaire, Curaçao, St. Maarten, and other islands, and it offers the Visit Caribbean Pass for travel between islands.

American Airlines offers daily nonstop service from New York and twice daily from San Juan. From Toronto and Montréal the flights are via San Juan. Continental Airlines has nonstop service twice a week from Houston. Delta flies nonstop daily from Atlanta. KLM offers regular service from Amsterdam. TWA has flights daily from San Juan.

➤ AIRLINES & CONTACTS: Air ALM (tel. 297/8–23546 on Aruba; 800/327–7230 in North America). American (tel. 297/8–22700 on Aruba; 800/433–7300 in North America). Continental (tel. 800/ 525–0280 in North America). Delta (tel. 297/8–80044 on Aruba; 800/241–4141 in North America). KLM (tel. 297/8–23546 on Aruba; 31/20–4–747–747 in Amsterdam). TWA (tel. 800/221–2000 in North America).

CHECK-IN AND BOARDING

Checking in, paying departure taxes (if they aren't included in your ticket), clearing security, and boarding can take time on Aruba. Since security has gotten tighter, **get to the airport at least 3 hours ahead of time.** You may be randomly selected for inspection of your carry-on baggage at the gate. Regulations prohibit certain items to be packed in your carry-on luggage, including batteries, cameras, cell phones, matches, lighters, and hand-held radios. Check with your hotel concierge before packing to return home.

Assuming that not everyone with a ticket will show up, airlines routinely overbook planes. When everyone does, airlines ask for volunteers to give up their seats. In return, these volunteers usually get a certificate for a free flight and are rebooked on the next flight out. If there are not enough volunteers, the airline must choose who will be denied boarding. The first to get bumped are passengers who checked in late and those flying on discounted tickets, so **get to the gate and check in as early as possible,** especially during peak periods.

Always **bring a government-issued photo I.D. to the airport;** even when it's not required, a passport is best.

FLYING TIMES
Aruba is 2½ hours from Miami, 4½ hours from New York, and 9½ hours from Amsterdam. The flight from New York to San Juan, Puerto Rico, takes 3½ hours; from Miami to San Juan it's 1½ hours; and from San Juan to Aruba it's just over an hour. Shorter still is the ¼- to ½-hour hop (depending on whether you take a prop or a jet plane) from Curaçao to Aruba.

RECONFIRMING
Check the status of your flight before you leave for the airport. You can do this on your carrier's Web site, by linking to a flight-status checker (many Web booking services offer these), or by calling your carrier or travel agent. Always confirm international flights at least 72 hours ahead of the scheduled departure time.

Be sure to **reconfirm your flights on smaller carriers.** You may be transferred to another flight if there are not enough passengers, or your plane may make unscheduled stops to pick up more clients or cargo. It's all part of the excitement—and unpredictability—of Caribbean travel. In addition, regional carriers usually have weight restrictions. Make sure to **travel light** or you could be subject to outrageous surcharges or be forced to put very large or heavy luggage on another flight.

Airport and Transfers

AIRPORT

Aruba's Aeropuerto Internacional Reina Beatrix (Queen Beatrix International Airport), near the island's south coast, underwent considerable renovations in 2001 that transformed it into a modern, passenger-friendly facility. There are new concession areas, business lounges, escalators, elevators, rest rooms, covered walkways, and baggage claim areas.

➤ **AIRPORT INFORMATION: Aeropuerto Internacional Reina Beatrix** (tel. 297/8–24800).

TRANSFERS

A taxi from the airport to most hotels takes about 20 minutes. It will cost about $16 to get to the hotels along Eagle Beach; $18 to the high-rise hotels on Palm Beach; and $9 to the hotels downtown. You'll find a taxi stand right outside the baggage claim area.

Business Hours

Bank hours are weekdays 8:15–5:45, with some branches closing for lunch from noon to 1. The Caribbean Mercantile Bank at the airport is open Saturday 9–4 and Sunday 9–1. The central post office in Oranjestad, catercorner from the San Francisco Church, is open weekdays 7:30–noon and 1–4:30. Shops are generally open Monday–Saturday 8:30–6. Some stores close for lunch hour from noon to 2. Many shops also open when cruise ships are in port on Sunday and holidays.

Bus Travel

Each day, from 6 AM to midnight, buses make hourly trips between the beach hotels and Oranjestad. The one-way fare is $1.15, while the roundtrip fare is $2. Exact change is preferred. Buses also run down the coast from Oranjestad to San Nicolas for the same fare. Contact the Aruba Tourism Authority for schedules.

Car Rental

You'll need a valid driver's license to rent a car, and you must meet the minimum age requirements of each rental service (Budget, for example, requires drivers to be over 25; Avis, between the ages of 23 and 70; and Hertz, over 21). A signed credit-card slip or a cash deposit of $500 is required. Rates for unlimited mileage are between $35 and $65 a day, with local agencies generally offering lower rates. Insurance is available starting at about $10 per day. Try to make reservations before arriving, and opt for a four-wheel-drive vehicle if you plan to explore the island.

AGENCIES: **Avis** (Kolibristraat 14, Oranjestad, tel. 297/8–28787; Airport, tel. 297/8–25496). **Budget** (Kolibristraat 1, Oranjestad, tel. 297/8–28600 or 800/472–3325). **Dollar** (Grendeaweg 15, Oranjestad, tel. 297/8–22783; Airport, tel. 297/8–25651; Manchebo Beach Resort, J. E. Irausquin Blvd. 55, tel. 297/8–26696). **Economy** (Kolibristraat 5, tel. 297/8–25176). **Hedwina Car Rental** (Bubali 93A, Noord, tel. 297/8–76442; Airport, tel. 297/8–30880). **Hertz** (Sabana Blanco 35, near the airport, tel. 297/8–21845; Airport, tel. 297/8–29112). **National** (Tanki Leendert 170, Noord, tel. 297/8–71967; Airport, tel. 297/8–25451). **Thrifty** (Balashi 65, Santa Cruz, tel. 297/8–55300; Airport, tel. 297/8–35335).

Car Travel

Most of Aruba's major attractions are fairly easy to find; others you'll happen upon only by sheer luck (or with an Aruban friend). Aside from the major highways, the island's winding roads are poorly marked (although the situation is slowly improving). International traffic signs and Dutch-style traffic signals (with an extra light for a turning lane) can be misleading if you're not used to them; use extreme caution, especially at intersections, until you grasp the rules of the road. Speed limits are rarely posted but are usually 80 kph (50 mph) in the countryside.

GASOLINE

Gas prices average $1 a liter (roughly ⅓ gallon), which is reasonable by Caribbean standards. Stations are plentiful in and near Oranjestad, San Nicolas, and Santa Cruz and near the major high-rise hotels on the western coast. All take cash (U.S. dollars or florins), and most take major credit cards.

PARKING

There aren't any parking meters in downtown Oranjestad, and finding an open spot is very difficult. Try the lot on Calle G. F. Betico Croes (across from the First National Bank), the one on Havenstraat near the Chez Matilde restaurant, or the one on Emanstraat near the water tower. Rates average $1.25 an hour.

Children on Aruba

Kids of all ages love the beach, which means they love Aruba. Resorts are increasingly sensitive to families' needs, and many now have playgrounds, extensive children's programs, and can arrange for baby-sitters. On sightseeing days try to **include some activities that will also interest your kids.** If you are renting a car, don't forget to **arrange for a car seat** when you reserve. For general advice about traveling with children, consult Fodor's FYI: *Travel with Your Baby* (available in bookstores everywhere).

FLYING

If your children are two or older, **ask about children's airfares.** As a general rule, infants under two not occupying a seat fly at greatly reduced fares or even for free. When booking, **confirm carry-on allowances** if you're traveling with infants. In general, for babies charged 10% of the adult fare you are allowed one carry-on bag and a collapsible stroller; if the flight is full, the stroller may have to be checked or you may be limited to less.

Experts agree that it's a good idea to use safety seats aloft for children weighing less than 40 pounds. Airlines set their own policies: U.S. carriers usually require that the child be ticketed, even if he or she is young enough to ride free, since the seats must be strapped into regular seats. Do check your airline's policy about using safety seats during takeoff and landing. Safety seats are not allowed everywhere in the plane, so get your seat assignments as early as possible.

When reserving, request children's meals or a freestanding bassinet (not available at all airlines) if you need them. But note that bulkhead seats, where you must sit to use the bassinet, may lack an overhead bin or storage space on the floor.

FOOD
Even if your youngsters are picky eaters, meals in the Caribbean shouldn't be a problem. Baby food is easy to find, and hamburgers and hot dogs are available at many resorts. Restaurant menus offer pasta, pizza, sandwiches, and ice cream. Supermarkets have cereal, snacks, and other packaged goods you'll recognize from home. At outdoor markets a few dollars will buy you enough bananas, mangoes, and other fresh fruit to last your entire vacation.

LODGING
Children are welcome in most Aruban resorts, and those under 12 or 16 can often stay free in their parents' room. Be sure to find out the cutoff age for children's discounts when booking.

PRECAUTIONS
To avoid immigration problems if your child has a different last name, bring identification that clarifies the family relationship (e.g., a birth certificate identifying the parent or a joint passport).

SUPPLIES AND EQUIPMENT

Suites at many resorts and even small hotels have hide-a-beds suitable for children sharing a parent's room. High chairs and cribs are also generally available. Supermarkets sell common brands of disposable diapers, baby food, and other necessities. Bookstores and souvenir shops have activity books and toys that kids will enjoy on vacation and back at home.

Cruise Travel

Cruising is a relaxed and convenient way to tour this beautiful part of the world: you get all of the amenities of a luxury hotel and enough activities to guarantee fun, even on rainy days. All your important decisions are made long before you board. Your itinerary is set, and you know the total cost of your vacation beforehand.

Ships usually call at several ports on a single voyage but are at each for only one day. Thus, although you may be exposed to several islands, you don't get much of a feel for any one of them. To learn how to plan, choose, and book a cruise-ship voyage, consult *Fodor's FYI: Plan & Enjoy Your Cruise* (available in bookstores everywhere).

➤ **CRUISE LINES: Carnival Cruise Lines** (3655 N.W. 87th Ave., Miami, FL 33178, tel. 305/599–2600 or 800/227–6482), **Celebrity Cruises** (1050 Caribbean Way, Miami, FL 33122), **Commodore/Crown Cruise Line** (4000 Hollywood Blvd., 385-S Tower, Hollywood, FL 33021, tel. 954/967–2100 or 800/832–1122), **Crystal Cruises** (2049 Century Park E, Suite 1400, Los Angeles, CA 90067, tel. 800/446–6620), **Cunard Line** (6100 Blue Lagoon Dr., Suite 400, Miami, FL 33126, tel. 800/221–4770), **Holland America Line** (300 Elliott Ave. W, Seattle, WA 98119, tel. 800/426–0327), **Norwegian Cruise Line** (95 Merrick Way, Coral Gables, FL 33134, tel. 800/327–7030), **Princess Cruises** (10100 Santa Monica Blvd., Los Angeles, CA 90067, tel. 310/553–1770 or 800/774–6237), **Radisson Seven Seas Cruises** (600 Corporate

Dr., Suite 410, Fort Lauderdale, FL 33334, tel. 800/333–3333), **Regal Cruises** (300 Regal Cruises Way, Box 1329, Palmetto, FL 34220, tel. 800/270–7245), **Royal Caribbean Cruise Line** (1050 Caribbean Way, Miami, FL 33132, tel. 800/327–6700), **Seabourn Cruise Line** (6100 Blue Lagoon Dr., Suite 400, Miami, FL 33126, tel. 800/929–9391), **Shipping Cruise Services, Ltd.** (75 Valencia Ave., Coral Gables, FL 33134, tel. 800/258–2633), **Star Clippers** (4101 Salzedo St., Coral Gables, FL 33146, tel. 800/442–0551), **Windstar Cruises** (300 Elliott Ave. W, Seattle, WA 98119, tel. 206/281–3535 or 800/258–7245).

➤ **ORGANIZATIONS: Cruise Lines International Association** (CLIA; 500 5th Ave., Suite 1407, New York, NY 10110, tel. 212/921–0066).

Customs and Duties

When shopping abroad, **keep receipts** for all purchases. Upon reentering the country, **be ready to show customs officials what you've bought.** If you feel a duty is incorrect, appeal the assessment. If you object to the way your clearance was handled, note the inspector's badge number. In either case, first ask to see a supervisor. If the problem isn't resolved, write to the appropriate authorities, beginning with the port director at your point of entry.

IN ARUBA

You can bring up to 1 liter of spirits, 3 liters of beer, or 2.25 liters of wine per person, and up to 200 cigarettes or 20 cigars. You don't need to declare the value of gifts or other items, although customs officials may inquire about large items or large quantities of items and charge (at their discretion) an import tax of 7.5% to 22% on items worth more than $230. Meat, birds, and illegal substances are forbidden. You may be asked to provide written verification that plants are free of diseases. If you're traveling with pets, bring a veterinarian's note attesting to their good health.

➤ **INFORMATION: Aruba Customs Office** (tel. 297/8–21800).

IN AUSTRALIA

Australian residents who are 18 or older may bring home A$400 worth of souvenirs and gifts (including jewelry), 250 cigarettes or 250 grams of tobacco, and 1,125 ml of alcohol (including wine, beer, and spirits). Residents under 18 may bring back A$200 worth of goods. Prohibited items include meat products. Seeds, plants, and fruits need to be declared upon arrival.

➤ **INFORMATION: Australian Customs Service** (Regional Director, Box 8, Sydney, NSW 2001, tel. 02/9213–2000, fax 02/9213–4000, www.customs.gov.au).

IN CANADA

Canadian residents who have been out of Canada for at least seven days may bring in C$750 worth of goods duty-free. If you've been away fewer than seven days but more than 48 hours, the duty-free allowance drops to C$200; if your trip lasts 24 to 48 hours, the allowance is C$50. You may not pool allowances with family members. Goods claimed under the C$750 exemption may follow you by mail; those claimed under the lesser exemptions must accompany you. Alcohol and tobacco products may be included in the seven-day and 48-hour exemptions but not in the 24-hour exemption. If you meet the age requirements of the province or territory through which you reenter Canada, you may bring in, duty-free, 1.5 liters of wine or 1.14 liters (40 imperial ounces) of liquor or 24 12-ounce cans or bottles of beer or ale. If you are 19 or older you may bring in, duty-free, 200 cigarettes and 50 cigars. Check ahead of time with the Canada Customs and Revenue Agency or the Department of Agriculture for policies regarding meat products, seeds, plants, and fruits.

You may send an unlimited number of gifts (only one gift per recipient, however) worth up to C$60 each duty-free to Canada. Label the package UNSOLICITED GIFT—VALUE UNDER $60. Alcohol and tobacco are excluded.

➤ **INFORMATION: Canada Customs and Revenue Agency** (2265 St. Laurent Blvd. S, Ottawa, Ontario K1G 4K3, tel. 204/983–3500; 506/636–5064; 800/461–9999 in Canada, www.ccra-adrc.gc.ca).

IN NEW ZEALAND

All homeward-bound residents may bring back NZ$700 worth of souvenirs and gifts; passengers may not pool their allowances, and children can claim only the concession on goods intended for their own use. For those 17 or older, the duty-free allowance also includes 4.5 liters of wine or beer; one 1,125-ml bottle of spirits; and either 200 cigarettes, 250 grams of tobacco, 50 cigars, or a combination of the three up to 250 grams. Meat products, seeds, plants, and fruits must be declared upon arrival to the Agricultural Services Department.

➤ **INFORMATION: New Zealand Customs** (Head Office, The Customhouse, 17–21 Whitmore St., Box 2218, Wellington, tel. 09/300–5399, www.customs.govt.nz).

IN THE U.K.

From countries outside the European Union you may bring home, duty-free, 200 cigarettes or 50 cigars; 1 liter of spirits or 2 liters of fortified or sparkling wine or liqueurs; 2 liters of still table wine; 60 ml of perfume; 250 ml of toilet water; plus £145 worth of other goods, including gifts and souvenirs. Prohibited items include meat products, seeds, plants, and fruits.

➤ **INFORMATION: HM Customs and Excise** (St. Christopher House, Southwark, London SE1 OTE, tel. 020/7928–3344, www.hmce.gov.uk).

IN THE U.S.

U.S. residents who have been out of the country for at least 48 hours and who have not used the $600 allowance or any part of it in the past 30 days may bring home $600 worth of foreign goods duty-free. This allowance, higher than the standard $400 exemption, applies to the 24 countries in the Caribbean Basin Initiative, including Aruba. If you visit a CBI country and a non-CBI country, you may still bring in $600 worth of goods duty-free, but no more than $400 may be from the non-CBI country. If you're returning from the U.S. Virgin Islands (USVI), the duty-free allowance is $1,200. If your travel included the USVI and another country—say, the Dominican Republic—the $1,200 allowance still applies, but at least $600 worth of goods must be from the USVI.

U.S. residents 21 and older may bring back 1 liter of alcohol duty-free. In addition, regardless of your age, you are allowed 200 cigarettes and 100 non-Cuban cigars. Antiques, which the U.S. Customs Service defines as objects more than 100 years old, enter duty-free, as do original works of art done entirely by hand, including paintings, drawings, and sculptures. You may also send packages home duty-free, with a limit of one parcel per addressee per day (except alcohol or tobacco products or perfume worth more than $5). You can mail up to $200 worth of goods for personal use; label the package PERSONAL USE and attach a list of its contents and their retail value. If the package contains your used personal belongings, mark it PERSONAL GOODS RETURNED to avoid paying duties. You may send up to $100 worth of goods as a gift; mark the package UNSOLICITED GIFT. Mailed items do not affect your duty-free allowance on your return.

➤ **INFORMATION: U.S. Customs Service** (for inquiries, 1300 Pennsylvania Ave. NW, Washington, DC 20229, www.customs. gov, tel. 202/354–1000; for complaints, Customer Satisfaction Unit, 1300 Pennsylvania Ave. NW, Room 5.5A, Washington, DC 20229; for registration of equipment, Office of Passenger Programs, 1300 Pennsylvania Ave. NW, Room 5.4D, Washington, DC 20229, tel. 202/927–0530).

Electricity

Aruba runs on a 110-volt cycle, the same as in the United States; outlets are usually the two-prong variety. Total blackouts are rare, and most large hotels have backup generators.

Emergencies

➤ **CONTACTS: Air Ambulance:** tel. 297/8–29197. **Ambulance and Fire:** tel. 115. **Hospital: Dr. Horacio Oduber Hospital** (L. G. Smith Blvd., across from Costa Linda Beach Resort and the Alhambra Bazaar and Casino, tel. 297/8–74300). **Botica Eagle Pharmacy** (L. G. Smith Blvd., near hospital, tel. 297/8–76103). **Police:** tel. 111000.

Etiquette and Behavior

It's best not to mention to residents how "American" everything is—many have settled here from South America and Europe. Aruba has a separate status with the Kingdom of the Netherlands, allowing it to handle its own aviation, customs, immigration, communications, and other internal matters, but the island does retain strong economic, cultural, and political ties with Holland.

Health

DIVERS' ALERT

Don't fly within 24 hours of scuba diving. In an emergency, Air Ambulance, run by Rupert Richard, will fly you to Curaçao at a low altitude if you need to get to a decompression chamber.

FOOD AND DRINK

As a rule, water is pure and food is wholesome in hotels and local restaurants throughout Aruba, but be cautious when buying food from street vendors. And just as you would at home, wash or peel all fruits and vegetables before eating them. Traveler's diarrhea, caused by consuming contaminated water, unpasteurized milk and milk products, and unrefrigerated food, isn't a big problem—unless it happens to you. So **watch what you eat,** especially at outdoor buffets in the hot sun. Make sure cooked food is hot and cold food has been properly refrigerated.

Mild cases of diarrhea may respond to Imodium (known generically as loperamide) or Pepto-Bismol (not as strong), both of which can be purchased in local pharmacies. Drink plenty of bottled water to keep from becoming dehydrated. A salt-sugar solution (½ teaspoon salt and 4 tablespoons sugar) per quart of water is a good remedy for rehydrating yourself.

PESTS AND OTHER HAZARDS

The major health risk is sunburn or sunstroke. A long-sleeve shirt, a hat, and long pants or a beach wrap are essential on a boat, for midday at the beach, and whenever you go out sightseeing. **Use sunscreen** with an SPF of at least 15— especially if you're fair—and apply it liberally on your nose, ears, and other sensitive and exposed areas. Make sure the sunscreen is waterproof if you're engaging in water sports. Always **limit your sun time** for the first few days and **drink plenty of liquids.** Limit intake of caffeine and alcohol, which hasten dehydration.

Mosquitoes and flies can be bothersome, so **pack strong repellent.** The strong trade winds are a relief in the subtropical climate, but don't hang your bathing suit on a balcony—it will probably blow away. Help Arubans conserve water and energy: turn off air-conditioning when you leave your room, and don't let water run unattended.

SHOTS AND MEDICATIONS

No special shots or vaccinations are required for Caribbean destinations.

➤ **HEALTH WARNINGS: National Centers for Disease Control** (CDC: National Center for Infectious Diseases, Division of Quarantine, Traveler's Health Section, 1600 Clifton Rd. NE, M/S

E-03, Atlanta, GA 30333, tel. 888/232–3228, fax 888/232–3299, www.cdc.gov).

Holidays

Aruba's official holidays include New Year's Day, Good Friday, Easter Sunday, and Christmas, as well as Betico Croes' Birthday (Jan. 25), Carnival Monday (Feb. 11 in 2002, March 3 in 2003, Feb. 23 in 2004), National Anthem and Flag Day (Mar. 18), Queen's Birthday (Apr. 30), Labor Day (May 1), Ascension Day (May 9), and Christmas (Dec. 25–26).

Lodging

Assume that hotels operate on the **European Plan** (EP, with no meals) unless we specify that they use the **Contintental Plan** (CP, with a Continental breakfast), **Modified American Plan** (MAP, with breakfast and dinner), or the **Full American Plan** (FAP, with all meals).

Mail and Shipping

You can send an airmail letter from Aruba to the United States or Canada (it will take 7–14 days) for Afl2 and a postcard for Afl1.15; a letter to Europe (2–3 weeks) is Afl1.75, a postcard Afl1. Prices to Australia and New Zealand (3–4 weeks) may be slightly higher. When addressing letters to Aruba, don't worry about the lack of formal addresses or postal codes; the island's postal service knows where to go.

If you need to send a package in a hurry, there are a few options to get the job done. The Federal Express office across from the airport offers overnight service to the United States if you get your package in before 3 PM. Another big courier service is UPS, and there are also several smaller local courier services that provide international deliveries, most of them open weekdays 9–5. Check the local phone book for details.

➤ **COURIER SERVICES: Federal Express** (Browninvest Financial Center, Wayaca 31-A, Oranjestad, tel. 297/9–29039). **UPS** (Rockefellerstraat 3, Oranjestad, tel. 297/8–28646).

Money Matters

CURRENCY

Arubans happily accept U.S. dollars virtually everywhere. That said, there's no real need to exchange money, except for necessary pocket change (for soda machines or pay phones). The official currency is the Aruban florin (Afl), also called the guilder, which is made up of 100 cents. Silver coins come in denominations of 1, 2½, 5, 10, 25, and 50 (the square one) cents. Paper currency comes in denominations of 5, 10, 25, 50, and 100 florins.

At press time exchange rates were Afl1.79 per U.S. dollar and Afl1.15 per Canadian dollar. Stores, hotels, and restaurants converted at Afl1.80; supermarkets and gas stations at Afl1.75. The Dutch Antillean florin—used on Bonaire and Curaçao—isn't accepted here. Prices quoted throughout this book are in U.S. dollars unless otherwise noted.

ATMS

If you need fast cash, you'll find ATMs that accept international cards (and dispense cash in the local currency) at banks in Oranjestad, at the major malls, and along the roads leading to the hotel strip.

➤ **BANKS: ABN/Amro Bank** (Caya G. F. Betico Croes 89, Oranjestad, tel. 297/8–21515). **Caribbean Mercantile Bank** (Caya G. F. Betico Croes 5, Oranjestad, tel. 297/8–23118).

CREDIT CARDS AND TRAVELER'S CHECKS

Major credit cards are widely accepted at hotels, restaurants, shops, car-rental agencies, and other service providers throughout Aruba. The only places that might not accept them are open-air markets or tiny shops in out-of-the-way villages.

It's smart to **write down the number of the credit cards you're carrying** and the toll-free number to call in case the card is lost or stolen.

Throughout this guide the following abbreviations are used: **AE**, American Express; **D**, Discover; **DC**, Diners Club; **MC**, MasterCard; and **V**, Visa.

SERVICE CHARGES, TIPPING AND TAXES

Hotels usually add an 11% service charge to the bill and collect a 6% government tax. Restaurants generally include a 10%–15% service charge on the bill; when in doubt, ask. If service isn't included, a 10% tip is standard; if it is included, it's still customary to add something extra, usually small change, at your discretion. Taxi drivers expect a 10%–15% tip, but it isn't mandatory. Porters and bellmen should receive about $2 per bag; chambermaids about $2 a day, but check to see if their tips are included in your bill so you don't overpay. The airport departure tax is a whopping $34.50, but the fee is usually included in your ticket price. Children under 2 don't pay departure tax. For purchases you'll pay a 6.5% ABB tax (a value-added tax) in all but the duty-free shops.

TRAVELER'S CHECKS

Get traveler's checks in small denominations—$20 or $50. Restaurants and most shops will accept them (with ID), and your hotel will cash them for you, though you might get change in local currency. In rural areas and small villages you'll need cash. Lost or stolen checks can usually be replaced within 24 hours. **Buy and pay for your own traveler's checks;** the person who bought the checks must request the refund.

Packing

Dress on Aruba is generally casual. **Bring loose-fitting clothing made of natural fabrics** to see you through days of heat and humidity. **Pack a beach cover-up,** both to protect yourself from the sun and to provide something to wear to and from your hotel room. Bathing suits and immodest attire are frowned upon away from the beach. A sun hat is advisable, but you don't have to pack one—inexpensive straw hats are available everywhere. For shopping and sightseeing, bring walking shorts, jeans, T-shirts, long-sleeve cotton shirts, slacks, and sundresses. Nighttime dress can range from very informal to casually elegant, depending on the establishment. A tie is practically never required, but a jacket may be appropriate in fancy restaurants. You may need a light sweater or jacket for evenings.

In your carry-on luggage, **pack an extra pair of eyeglasses or contact lenses** (but if you forget, there are several eye-care centers in town where you can pick up a spare pair of lenses) and **enough of any medication you take** to last the entire trip. You may also ask your doctor to write a spare prescription using the drug's generic name, since brand names may vary from country to country. In luggage to be checked, **never pack prescription drugs or valuables.** To avoid customs delays, carry medications in their original packaging. And don't forget to carry with you the addresses of offices that handle refunds of lost traveler's checks.

CHECKING LUGGAGE
You are allowed one carry-on bag and one personal article, such as a purse or a laptop computer. Make sure that everything you carry aboard will fit under your seat or in the overhead bin. Get to the gate early, so you can board as soon as possible, before the overhead bins fill up.

If you are flying internationally, note that baggage allowances may be determined not by piece but by weight—generally 88 pounds (40 kilograms) in first class, 66 pounds (30 kilograms) in business class, and 44 pounds (20 kilograms) in economy.

Before departure, **itemize your bags' contents** and their worth, and label the bags with your name, address, and phone number.

(If you use your home address, cover it so potential thieves can't see it readily.) Inside each bag, **pack a copy of your itinerary**. At check-in, **make sure that each bag is correctly tagged** with the destination airport's three-letter code. If your bags arrive damaged or fail to arrive at all, file a written report with the airline before leaving the airport.

Passports

When traveling internationally, **carry your passport** even if you don't need one (it's always the best form of I.D.) and **make two photocopies of the data page** (one for someone at home and another for you, carried separately from your passport). If you lose your passport, promptly call the nearest embassy or consulate and the local police.

U.S. passport applications for children under age 14 require consent from both parents or legal guardians; both parents must appear together to sign the application. If only one parent appears, he or she must submit a written statement from the other parent authorizing passport issuance for the child. A parent with sole authority must present evidence of it when applying; acceptable documentation includes the child's certified birth certificate listing only the applying parent, a court order specifically permitting this parent's travel with the child, or a death certificate for the non-applying parent. Application forms and instructions are available on the Web site of the U.S. State Department's Bureau of Consular Affairs (www.travel.state.gov).

ENTERING ARUBA

U.S. and Canadian citizens need a valid passport or a birth certificate with a raised seal and a government-issued photo ID. Visitors from the member countries of the European Union must also carry their European Union Travel Card, as well as a passport. All other nationalities must have a valid passport.

PASSPORT OFFICES

The best time to apply for a passport or to renew is in fall and winter. Before any trip check your passport's expiration date and, if necessary, renew it as soon as possible.

➤ **AUSTRALIAN CITIZENS: Australian Passport Office** (tel. 131–232, www.dfat.gov.au/passports).

➤ **CANADIAN CITIZENS: Passport Office** (tel. 819/994–3500 or 800/567–6868, www.dfait-maeci.gc.ca/passport).

➤ **NEW ZEALAND CITIZENS: New Zealand Passport Office** (tel. 04/494–0700, www.passports.govt.nz).

➤ **U.K. CITIZENS: London Passport Office** (tel. 0990/210–410) for fees and documentation requirements and for an emergency passport.

➤ **U.S. CITIZENS: National Passport Information Center** (tel. 900/225–5674; calls are 35¢ per minute for automated service, $1.05 per minute for operator service).

Rest Rooms

Outside of Oranjestad, the only public rest rooms you'll find will be in one of the few restaurants that dot the countryside.

Safety

Arubans are very friendly, so you needn't be afraid to stop and ask anyone for directions. It's a relatively safe island, but common-sense rules still apply. Lock your rental car when you leave it, and leave valuables in your hotel safe. Don't leave bags unattended in the airport, on the beach, or on tour vehicles.

Shopping

For many, shopping on Aruba means duty-free bargains on jewelry, designer clothing, china, crystal, and other luxury goods from around the world. At the Aruba Trading Company in the airport departure hall (near U.S. immigration), you'll find a complete selection of duty-free liquors, tobacco, and perfumes. For others, shopping means buying locally produced crafts and works of art.

Bargaining isn't expected in shops, but at open-air markets and with street vendors it may be acceptable. Keep in mind, however, that selling handicrafts or home-grown produce may be a local's only livelihood. When bargaining, consider the amount of work or effort involved and the item's value to you. Vendors don't set artificially high prices and then expect to bargain; they bargain so you'll buy from them instead of their neighbor.

Taxis

There's a dispatch office at the airport; you can also flag down taxis on the street (look for license plates with a "TX" tag). Rates are fixed (i.e., there are no meters; the rates are set by the government and displayed on a chart), though you and the driver should agree on the fare before your ride begins. Add $1 to the fare after midnight and $1–$3 on Sunday and holidays. An hour-long island tour costs about $30, with up to four people. Rides into town from Eagle Beach run about $5; from Palm Beach, about $8.

➤ **TAXI SERVICE: Airport Taxi Dispatch** (tel. 297/8–22116).

Telephones

To call Aruba direct from the United States, dial 011–297–8, followed by the five-digit number in Aruba. (To call from elsewhere abroad, substitute 011 with the country of origin's international access code.) International, direct, and operator-assisted calls from Aruba are possible to all countries in the world via hotel operators or from the Government Long Distance Telephone, Telegraph, and Radio Office (SETAR), in the post-office building in Oranjestad. When making calls on Aruba, simply dial the five-digit number. AT&T customers can dial 800–8000 from special phones at the cruise dock and in the airport's arrival and departure halls. From other phones dial 121 to contact the SETAR International Operator to place a collect or AT&T calling card call. Local calls from pay phones, which accept both local currency and phone cards, cost 25¢. Business travelers or vacationers who need to be in regular contact with their families at home can rent an international cell phone from the concierge in most hotels or at some local electronics stores.

Tours and Packages

Because everything is prearranged on a prepackaged tour or independent vacation, you spend less time planning—and often get it all at a good price.

BOOKING WITH AN AGENT

Travel agents are excellent resources. But it's a good idea to collect brochures from several agencies, as some agents' suggestions may be influenced by relationships with tour and package firms that reward them for volume sales. If you have a special interest, **find an agent with expertise in that area**; the American Society of Travel Agents (ASTA; ☞ Travel Agencies) has a database of specialists worldwide.

Make sure your travel agent knows the accommodations and other services of the place being recommended. Ask about the hotel's location, room size, beds, and whether it has a pool, room service, or programs for children, if you care about these. Has your agent been there in person or sent others whom you can contact?

Do some homework on your own, too: local tourism boards can provide information about lesser-known and small-niche operators, some of which may sell only direct.

BUYER BEWARE

Each year consumers are stranded or lose their money when tour operators—even large ones with excellent reputations—go out of business. So check out the operator. Ask several travel agents about its reputation, and try to book with a company that has a consumer-protection program. (Look for information in the company's brochure.) In the United States, members of the National Tour Association and the United States Tour Operators Association are required to set aside funds to cover your payments and travel arrangements in the event that the company defaults. It's also a good idea to choose a company that participates in the American Society of Travel Agents' Tour Operator Program (TOP); ASTA will act as mediator in any disputes between you and your tour operator.

Remember that the more your package or tour includes the better you can predict the ultimate cost of your vacation. Make sure you know exactly what is covered, and beware of hidden costs. Are taxes, tips, and transfers included? Entertainment and excursions? These can add up.

➤ TOUR-OPERATOR RECOMMENDATIONS: American Society of Travel Agents (☞ Travel Agencies). National Tour Association (NTA; 546 E. Main St., Lexington, KY 40508, tel. 859/226–4444 or 800/682–8886, www.ntaonline.com). United States Tour Operators Association (USTOA; 275 Madison Ave., Suite 2014, New York, NY 10016, tel. 212/599–6599 or 800/468–7862, fax 212/599–6744, www.ustoa.com).

ISLAND TOURS

If you try a cruise around the island, know that the choppy waters are stirred up by trade winds and that catamarans are much smoother than single-hulled boats. Sucking on a peppermint or lemon candy may help a queasy stomach; avoid boating with an empty or overly full stomach. Moonlight cruises cost about $25 per person. There are also a variety of snorkeling, dinner and dancing, and sunset party cruises to choose from, priced from $25 to $60 per person. Many of the smaller operators work out of their homes; they often offer to pick you up (and drop you off) at your hotel or meet you at particular hotel pier.

Explore an underwater reef teeming with marine life without getting wet. Atlantis Submarines operates a 20-m (65-ft) air-conditioned sub that takes 48 passengers 29–46 m (95–150 ft) below the surface along Barcadera Reef. The two-hour trip (including boat transfer to the submarine platform and 50-minute plunge) costs $72. Make reservations one day in advance. Another option is the *Seaworld Explorer*, a semisubmersible that allows you to view Aruba's marine habitat from 2 m (6 ft) below the surface. The cost is $35 for a 1½-hour tour.

You can see the main sights in one day, but set aside two days to really meander. Guided tours are your best option if you have only a short time. Aruba's Transfer Tour & Taxi C.A. takes you to the main sights on personalized tours that cost $30 per hour.

De Palm Tours has a near monopoly on Aruban sightseeing; you can make reservations through its general office or at hotel tour-desk branches. The company's basic 3½-hour tour hits the highlights. Wear tennis or hiking shoes, and bring a lightweight jacket or wrap (the air-conditioned bus gets cold). It begins at 9:30 AM, picks you up in your hotel lobby, and costs $22.50 per person. A full-day Jeep Adventure tour ($59.50 per person) takes you to sights that would be difficult for you to find on your own. Bring a bandanna to cover your mouth; the ride on rocky dirt roads can get dusty. De Palm also offers full-day tours of Curaçao ($219; every Friday). Prices include round-trip airfare, transfers, sightseeing, and lunch; there's free time for shopping.

Romantic horse-drawn-carriage rides through the city streets of Oranjestad run $30 for a 30-minute tour; hours of operation are 7 PM–11 PM, and carriages depart from the clock tower at the Royal Plaza Mall.

➤ **BOAT TOUR OPERATORS: Atlantis Submarines** (Seaport Village Marina, tel. 297/8–36090). **De Palm Tours** (L. G. Smith Blvd. 142, Oranjestad, tel. 297/8–24400 or 800/766–6016, www.depalm.com). **Pelican Tours & Watersports** (J. E. Irausquin Blvd. 232, Oranjestad, tel. 297/8–72302, www.pelican-aruba.com). **Red Sail Sports** (Seaport Village Mall, L. G. Smith Blvd. 82, Oranjestad, tel. 297/8–61603; 877/733–7245 in the U.S., www.aruba-redsail.com). **Seaworld Explorer** (tel. 297/8–62416).

➤ **ORIENTATION TOUR OPERATORS: Aruba's Transfer Tour & Taxi** (Pos Abao 41, Oranjestad, tel. 297/8–22116). **De Palm Tours** (L. G. Smith Blvd. 142, Oranjestad, tel. 297/8–24400 or 800/766–6016, www.depalm.com).

Travel Agencies

A good travel agent puts your needs first. Look for an agency that has been in business at least five years, emphasizes customer service, and has someone on staff who specializes in your destination. In addition, **make sure the agency belongs to a professional trade organization.** The American Society of Travel Agents (ASTA)—the largest and most influential in the field with more than 24,000 members in some 140 countries—maintains and enforces a strict code of ethics and will step in to help mediate any agent-client disputes involving ASTA members if necessary. ASTA (whose motto is "Without a travel agent, you're on your own") also maintains a Web site that includes a directory of agents. (If a travel agency is also acting as your tour operator, *see* Buyer Beware in Tours & Packages.)

➤ **LOCAL AGENT REFERRALS: American Society of Travel Agents** (ASTA; 1101 King St., Suite 200, Alexandria, VA 22314, tel.

800/965–2782 24-hr hot line, fax 703/739–3268, www.astanet. com). **Association of British Travel Agents** (68–71 Newman St., London W1T 3AH, tel. 020/7637–2444, fax 020/7637–0713, www.abtanet.com). **Association of Canadian Travel Agents** (130 Albert St., Suite 1705, Ottawa, Ontario K1P 5G4, tel. 613/237–3657, fax 613/237–7052, www.acta.net). **Australian Federation of Travel Agents** (Level 3, 309 Pitt St., Sydney, NSW 2000, tel. 02/9264–3299, fax 02/9264–1085, www.afta.com.au). **Travel Agents' Association of New Zealand** (Level 5, Tourism and Travel House, 79 Boulcott St., Box 1888, Wellington 10033, tel. 04/499–0104, fax 04/499–0827, www.taanz.org.nz).

Time

Aruba is in the Atlantic Standard Time zone, which is one hour later than Eastern Standard Time or four hours earlier than Greenwich mean time. During Daylight Saving Time, between April and October, Atlantic Standard is the same time as Eastern Daylight Time.

Visitor Information

Before leaving home, contact the Aruba Tourism Authority at one of its many offices. The Caribbean Tourism Organization (CTO) is another good resource. On Aruba the tourist office has free brochures and information officers who are ready to answer any questions you may have, weekdays 7:30–4:30.

➤ **ARUBA INFORMATION: Aruba Tourism Authority** (tel. 800/ 862–7822, www.arubatourism.com; L. G. Smith Blvd. 172, Eagle Beach, Aruba, tel. 297/8–23777; 1 Financial Plaza, Suite 136, Fort Lauderdale, FL 33394, tel. 954/767–6477; 3455 Peach Tree Rd. NE, Suite 500, Atlanta, GA 30326, tel. 404/892–7822; 5901 N. Cicero, Suite 301, Chicago, IL, 60646, tel. 773/202–5054; 1000 Harbor Blvd., Ground Level, Weehawken, NJ 07087, tel. 201/ 330–0800; 12707 North Freeway, Suite 138, Houston, TX 77060-

1234, tel. 281/872–7822; Business Centre 5875, Suite 201, Hwy. 7, Vaughan, Ontario, L4L 8Z7, tel. 905/264–3434).

➤ **CARIBBEAN-WIDE INFORMATION: Caribbean Tourism Organization** (80 Broad St., New York, NY 10004, tel. 212/635–9530, www.caribtourism.com; Vigilant House, 120 Wilton Rd., London SW1V 1JZ, tel. 020/7233–8382).

➤ **U.S. GOVERNMENT ADVISORIES: U.S. Department of State** (Overseas Citizens Services Office, Room 4811 N.S., 2201 C St. NW, Washington, DC 20520, tel. 202/647–5225 for interactive hot line, 301/946–4400 computer bulletin board, fax 202/647–3000 interactive hot line); enclose a self-addressed, stamped business-size envelope.

Web Sites

Do check out the World Wide Web when you're planning. You'll find everything from up-to-date weather forecasts to virtual tours of famous cities. Fodor's Web site, www.fodors.com, is a great place to start your on-line travels.

One of the most helpful sites about Aruba may very well be the island's own www.aruba.com. For information on the Caribbean, visit one of the following: www.caribtourism.com (the Caribbean Tourism Organization's official site, with many island-specific links); www.caribbeanchannel.com (with information presented both thematically and by island); www.caribbeantravel.com (the official Caribbean Hotel Association site); www.caribbeancyberspace.com (for general information and good links); www.caribbeannewspapers.com (with links to newspapers published throughout the Caribbean); www.caribinfo.com (with a directory of Web sites based in or related to the Caribbean and links to local phone directories); www2.prestel.co.uk/caribbean (with aviation routes and schedules as well as links to all airlines that serve the region); www.cruising.org (the Cruise Lines International Association's site, with many ship profiles); www.cananews.com and www.cweek.com (for Caribbean news).

When to Go

Aruba's high season is traditionally winter—from December 15 to April 14—when northern weather is at its worst. During this season you're guaranteed the most entertainment at resorts and the most people with whom to enjoy it. It's also the most fashionable, the most expensive, and the most popular time to visit—and most hotels are heavily booked. You must make reservations at least two or three months in advance for the very best places. Hotel prices drop 20%–40% after April 15; cruise prices also fall.

➤ **FORECASTS: Weather Channel Connection** (tel. 900/932–8437), 95¢ per minute from a Touch-Tone phone.

index

Fodor's
Key to the Guides

America's guidebook leader publishes guides for every kind of traveler. Check out our many series and find your perfect match.

Fodor's Gold Guides

America's favorite travel-guide series offers the most detailed insider reviews of hotels, restaurants, and attractions in all price ranges, plus great background information, smart tips, and useful maps.

Fodor's Road Guide USA

Big guides for a big country—the most comprehensive guides to America's roads, packed with places to stay, eat, and play across the U.S.A. Just right for road warriors, family vacationers, and cross-country trekkers.

COMPASS AMERICAN GUIDES

Stunning guides from top local writers and photographers, with gorgeous photos, literary excerpts, and colorful anecdotes. A must-have for culture mavens, history buffs, and new residents.

Fodor's CITYPACKS

Concise city coverage with a foldout map. The right choice for urban travelers who want everything under one cover.

Fodor's EXPLORING GUIDES

Hundreds of color photos bring your destination to life. Lively stories lend insight into the culture, history, and people.

Fodor's POCKET GUIDES

For travelers who need only the essentials. The best of Fodor's in pocket-size packages for just $9.95.

Fodor's To Go
Credit-card–size, magnetized color microguides that fit in the palm of your hand—perfect for "stealth" travelers or as gifts.

Fodor's FLASHMAPS
Every resident's map guide. 60 easy-to-follow maps of public transit, parks, museums, zip codes, and more.

Fodor's CITYGUIDES
Sourcebooks for living in the city: Thousands of in-the-know listings for restaurants, shops, sports, nightlife, and other city resources.

Fodor's AROUND THE CITY WITH KIDS
68 great ideas for family days, recommended by resident parents. Perfect for exploring in your own backyard or on the road.

Fodor's ESCAPES
Fill your trip with once-in-a-lifetime experiences, from ballooning in Chianti to overnighting in the Moroccan desert. These full-color dream books point the way.

Fodor's FYI
Get tips from the pros on planning the perfect trip. Learn how to pack, fly hassle-free, plan a honeymoon or cruise, stay healthy on the road, and travel with your baby.

Fodor's Languages for Travelers
Practice the local language before hitting the road. Available in phrase books, cassette sets, and CD sets.

Karen Brown's Guides
Engaging guides to the most charming inns and B&Bs in the U.S.A. and Europe, with easy-to-follow inn-to-inn itineraries.

Baedeker's Guides
Comprehensive guides, trusted since 1829, packed with A–Z reviews and star ratings.

FODOR'S POCKET ARUBA

EDITOR: Mark Sullivan

Editorial Contributors: Karen W. Bressler and Elise Rosen

Editorial Production: Ira-Neil Dittersdorf

Maps: David Lindroth, *cartographer;* Bob Blake and Rebecca Baer, *map editors*

Design: Fabrizio La Rocca, *creative director;* Tigist Getachew, *art director;* Melanie Marin, *photo editor*

Production/Manufacturing: Angela L. McLean

Cover Photograph: Darrell Jones/AllStock/PictureQuest

Second Edition

ISBN 1–4000–1067–5

ISSN 1098–2663

IMPORTANT TIP

Although all prices, opening times, and other details in this book are based on information supplied to us at press time, changes occur all the time in the travel world, and Fodor's cannot accept responsibility for facts that become outdated or for inadvertent errors or omissions. So **always confirm information when it matters,** especially if you're making a detour to visit a specific place.

SPECIAL SALES

Fodor's Travel Publications are available at special discounts for bulk purchases for sales promotions or premiums. Special editions, including personalized covers, excerpts of existing guides, and corporate imprints, can be created in large quantities for special needs. For more information, contact your local bookseller or write to Special Markets, Fodor's Travel Publications, 1745 Broadway, New York, NY 10019. Inquiries from Canada should be directed to your local Canadian bookseller or sent to Random House of Canada, Ltd., Marketing Department, 2775 Matheson Boulevard East, Mississauga, Ontario L4W 4P7. Inquiries from the United Kingdom should be sent to Fodor's Travel Publications, 20 Vauxhall Bridge Road, London SW1V 2SA, England.

PRINTED IN THE UNITED STATES OF AMERICA

10 9 8 7 6 5 4 3 2 1